The Dream Lives On:

A Journey Through Fire, Faith, and the
Fulfillment of God's Call

Revised and Expanded Edition

Author – Eld Joel Latimore Jr.

The Dream Lives On:

A Journey Through Fire, Faith, and the
Fulfillment of God's Call
Revised and Expanded Edition

Written by Eld Joel Latimore Jr.

© 2026 Eld Joel Latimore Jr.

ISBN (paperback): 979-8-218-84543-8

Latimore Publishing

Scripture quotations are taken from the King
James Version (KJV) of the Bible, unless
otherwise noted.

Table of Contents

- Dedication

- Author's Note

- Preface

Dedication

To every servant of God who has carried a dream through dark seasons…

To the minister who stayed faithful while misunderstood…

To the leader who poured into others while feeling empty themselves…

To the dreamers who were betrayed by the very ones they loved…

And to those who almost gave up— but didn't.

This book is for you.

May the life of Joseph remind you that the dream does not die—and neither should your ministry. God is not finished with you yet.

And to every dreamer who has grown through the fire since these words were first written—this edition is for you.

— Elder Joel Latimore Jr.

Author's Note (Expanded Edition)

Since the first release of The Dream Lives On, I have continued to walk through seasons of refinement and revelation. Each trial and triumph has deepened my understanding of God's purpose and grace.

This Revised and Expanded Edition includes new insights, reflections, and wisdom keys that the Lord has revealed since these pages were first written. My prayer is that every reader will not only be inspired but strengthened to endure and believe again — because the dream still lives on.

With love and purpose,

Elder Joel Latimore Jr.

Preface (Revised and Expanded Edition)

When The Dream Lives On was first written, it was birthed out of seasons of *silence, struggle, and surrender.* In those early pages, I could only see fragments of what God was doing. Since then, He has proven Himself faithful through *new fires, deeper revelations,* and *unexpected victories.*

This Revised and Expanded Edition carries the wisdom gathered along the way—lessons learned in quiet rooms, revelations born in waiting, and insight refined through endurance.

Though the dream has not changed, its depth has grown. And if you are reading these words, it is because God is still writing the next chapter of your story. The dream still lives, and so must you.

Because every dreamer who refuses to quit becomes living proof that the dream still lives on

— **Elder Joel Latimore Jr.**

Introduction

Let me begin by saying that the Bible does not tell us in detail what Jacob taught Joseph and his brothers during their formative years. But we do know this—Jacob was not an ordinary man. He had wrestled with God and prevailed. He was a man of *vision, wisdom, and strategy*.

A shrewd businessman who had survived under Laban's manipulation, Jacob had learned the value of *discernment, hard work, and divine covenant.*

It's reasonable to believe that Joseph—being the son of Jacob's old age—witnessed much of this firsthand.

The text reveals that Joseph was mature beyond his years. At just seventeen, he was already trusted with responsibility and had the moral courage to report evil deeds.

He was not naive. He was *observant.* He was *insightful.* Though young, he was not easily manipulated or swayed by the crowd.

There was something in him that stood apart from his brothers. He may not have known what the dream meant in full, but he was no fool. He was discerning, and his life reflected the residue of a father who had walked with God.

It is within this backdrop that **Genesis 37** opens—a chapter filled with complexity, calling, and conflict.

Joseph is introduced not just as a dreamer, but as a young man with a distinct favor on his life. His relationship with his father Jacob was special.

Jacob loved him more than all his other sons, and this was not merely parental affection—it was prophetic recognition.

Jacob saw something in Joseph that mirrored his own Spiritual encounters. He made Joseph a coat of many colors, signifying favor, authority, and distinction.

Jacob's love for Joseph was not just emotional—it was prophetic. But prophetic favor often carries a heavy price. The same coat that marked Joseph for honor also marked him for hostility.

His brothers didn't just hate his dreams; they hated what his father's favor represented—God's hand choosing someone among them.

We must be careful when we are favored by someone as anointed or discerning as Jacob.

Favor without maturity can draw warfare we are not yet equipped to handle. Sometimes divine preference feels like punishment before it becomes promotion. God uses favor not to inflate us, but to expose what still needs refining.

Joseph's story warns us that favor will test our humility before it confirms our destiny. And what looks like unfair rejection may actually be divine protection, positioning us for revelation we could not yet carry at home.

This was not just a garment—it was a mark. A visible sign that Joseph was set apart.

But with favor comes friction. The coat attracted jealousy, and the dream incited hatred. But here lies a divine **wisdom key:** *every dreamer must understand that Favor will always draw fire—it attracts resistance, but it also proves readiness.*

Not everyone who celebrates your calling understands its cost.

Every dream has a birthplace. For Joseph, it began in **Genesis 37.** He was seventeen, inexperienced, and unprepared for what was coming—but the dream was real.

What makes Joseph's story so remarkable is that many tried to kill the dream—but the dream refused to die.

His brothers mocked him, plotted against him, and cast him into a pit. Potiphar's wife falsely accused him. The butler forgot him. And yet, every act of opposition only pushed the dream closer to its fulfillment.

But Joseph didn't know this when the dream first came. He had no idea that the promise would demand such a price.

He didn't know that being chosen would mean being targeted. The dream seemed glorious, but he could not foresee the cost—the *betrayal* of his own brothers, the *humiliation* of being sold into slavery, or the *agony* of being falsely imprisoned for a crime he didn't commit.

He didn't anticipate that obedience to God could lead to rejection by man, or that purity could provoke persecution. And yet, it was all part of God's divine preparation.

What Joseph endured was not punishment—it was refinement. Each obstacle was an instrument in God's hand, crafting him into the kind of man who could carry the weight of the dream.

The pit stripped him of *pride*. Potiphar's house taught him *stewardship*. The prison tested his *patience* and deepened his *discernment*. And when the time came to stand before Pharaoh, Joseph was no longer just a favored son—he was a seasoned vessel.

Everything he endured had trained him for *rulership, compassion, and wisdom.* His suffering was the schoolroom that prepared him to save a nation.

Here's the part we often miss: *the dream did not just survive for Joseph's benefit—it lived on to bless the very ones who tried to destroy it.*

When famine struck, it was Joseph—the dreamer they rejected—who became the vessel of their survival. The very people who tried to silence him had to kneel before him. What they meant for evil, God used for good, not only to elevate Joseph, but to preserve a nation.

The story of Joseph is not just a Bible story—it is a divine pattern. It's proof that:

- God speaks in visions.

- Enemies can't cancel divine assignments.

- The process is painful, but the outcome is purposeful.

I know what it feels like to carry a dream that no one believes in—not even you at times. I know what it feels like to wonder if what God showed you will ever come to pass.

But I've come to tell you: that the dream lives on and does not die. It may go underground. It may be delayed. But if God gave it—He will resurrect it.

This book is a walk with Joseph. It is a walk-through *betrayal, false accusation, disappointment, and ultimately, divine fulfillment.*

It is a book for every dreamer who has been discouraged by the process.

This book is also filled with wisdom keys— principles that unlock the mystery of your journey. I won't tell you everything will be easy. But I will tell you—it will be worth it.

Let's begin in **Genesis 37.**

Before we move forward, let us pause and take a closer look at the foundation of Joseph's story. Hidden within **Genesis 37** are the *patterns, principles, and providence* that reveal how God works through *favor, family,* and *fire* to shape the dreamer.

A Closer Look at Genesis 37

Before we walk through Joseph's journey, it's important to pause and examine the foundation where his story begins. **Genesis 37** is not only the opening of Joseph's life—it is the divine stage where purpose, pain, and providence first collide.

The name Joseph comes from the Hebrew root *yasaf*, meaning **"to add," "to continue,"** or **"to increase."**

When Rachel named him, she declared, *"The Lord shall add to me another son"* **(Genesis 30:24).** Yet in prophetic symbolism, Joseph's name speaks beyond his birth—it represents *continuation, extension, and divine increase.*

His life would literally add to the covenant line, preserving the nation through which God's promise would continue.

Nothing in Joseph's story is accidental. Every event in **Genesis 37**—*his dreams, his coat, his brothers' jealousy, his descent into the pit—is woven by divine design.* What looks like chaos is actually covenant continuity.

Bible Study Framework: Observing Genesis 37

Observation – What do you see?

Genesis 37 divides naturally into three movements:

1. **Verses 1–11:** Joseph's dream and his father's favor.

2. **Verses 12–24:** The brothers' envy and betrayal.

3. **Verses 25–36:** Joseph's descent and deception.

Key repeated words: *brothers, dream, hate, strip, pit.* Each repetition reveals the tension between human jealousy and divine purpose.

Favor, Family Dynamics, and God's Election

Genesis 37 makes two truths run side by side: **human favoritism** and **divine election.** Jacob's visible favoritism toward Joseph—symbolized by the **special coat** and a **greater degree of love (Gen. 37:3)**—creates a combustible environment at home. Joseph's **dreams** then announce a future in which his brothers will bow, intensifying their **jealousy and hatred (Gen. 37:5–11).**

From the brothers' perspective, Joseph looks "set up" to rule over them; from heaven's perspective, God is positioning a servant to **save his family and others** in the famine to come **(Gen. 45:5–8; 50:20).**

Key Observations about Favor and Fire

- **The coat marks distinction** (favor, authority, assignment) but also paints a target. Public honor can provoke private hostility.

- **Dreams disclose destiny, not timing.** Joseph received a true word, but not yet the wisdom or maturity to carry it.

- **Human favoritism wounds community.**
  Jacob's partiality seeds resentment;
  unhealed family dynamics become Satan's
  leverage.

- **Divine election overrules human intent.**
  Even when favor attracts fire, God bends
  opposition toward preparation.

Pastoral Warning: Being Favored Can Be Costly

We must be careful when favored by someone as
powerful and anointed as Jacob. **Borrowed
favor** (favor conferred by people) can **open
doors** but also **paint targets** you are not yet
ready to carry.

If your **character** is not growing at the pace of your **visibility,** favor can threaten your livelihood—relationships, reputation, opportunities, even your safety.

Wisdom Keys

1. **Favor requires formation.** Seek depth before platforms; let obscurity build the muscle that honor will demand.

2. **Honor quietly.** Not every dream needs public airtime. Share revelations with the right people at the right time.

3. **Expect friction.** Divine distinction will often draw resistance; let resistance refine, not embitter, you.

4. **Discern sources of favor.** Distinguish **human favoritism** (which is partial and fragile) from God's favor (which is purifying and purposeful).

5. **Guard your livelihood.** When elevated by influential leaders, establish boundaries, accountability, and spiritual covering so the **weight of favor** doesn't crush your future.

Application

- If you carry visible favor, pursue hidden faithfulness—prayer, service, integrity, and teachability.

- Invite mentors who will correct you privately so God can promote you safely.

- When your dream agitates others, stay gentle and steady; let God do the explaining in His time.

- Pray: *"Lord, grow my character as fast as You grow my influence."*

Interpretation – What did it mean then?

To ancient readers, this was not merely a family drama—it was a demonstration of divine providence. God's covenant promises to Abraham *("in you all nations shall be blessed")* was still alive, even in the dysfunction of Jacob's household.

Joseph becomes the next vessel of preservation. His suffering secures the covenant's survival.

Theological Principle – What does it mean for us today?

God's providence often hides behind human failure.

The pit does not cancel the promise—it activates it.

The betrayal that seems to bury the dream becomes the very soil where it grows.

Application – How should we respond?

- View every test as training for purpose.

- Remember that divine favor attracts resistance—but also refinement.

- Recognize that what others mean for evil, God reworks for good.

- Trust that yasaf—the God who adds—will increase and continue His plan in you.

Wisdom Key: Every dreamer must learn that divine providence often travels through human pain. What looks like loss is often the very thing God uses to position you for increase.

Chapter 1: The Dream Giver

"And Joseph dreamed a dream, and he told it his brethren: and they hated him yet the more."

— Genesis 37:5

Not every dream is divine, and not every vision is from God. But when God sends one—whether by night or by open revelation—it carries weight.

A divine *dream* or *vision* will not flatter your ego; it will stretch your faith. The dreams that come from self-ambition inflate the heart; the ones that come from God enlarge it.

Self-born visions demand attention; God-given visions demand surrender. It will not spare your comfort; it will provoke your crucifixion.

God often reveals the glory but withholds the grind. He gives the vision but conceals the valley that leads to its fulfillment.

God does not only speak through dreams; He also speaks through visions. Dreams often come in the stillness of rest, but visions arrive in the stillness of surrender.

Both are divine languages of revelation used to unveil destiny and direct purpose. Whether asleep or awake, God has always used *imagery, symbols*, and *insight* to prepare His chosen vessels for what lies ahead.

Just as He gave Joseph a dream, He gave **Ezekiel** a vision of dry bones, **Isaiah** a vision of the Lord high and lifted up, and **Peter** a vision that opened the door of salvation to the Gentiles.

Different vessels, different methods — but the same God. **The Dream Giver** is also the Vision Revealer, and His intent is always redemptive.

Many who carry a vision wrestle with the same struggles as Joseph: *rejection, isolation,* and *misunderstanding.* Sometimes those around you can't see what you've seen or hear what you've heard, and the loneliness of revelation becomes its own fire. Yet the testing of that vision is what confirms its authenticity.

When God entrusts you with revelation — whether *a dream, a vision,* or *a word* — He is not just giving you information; He's forming you into a vessel that can live out that revelation. Visions, like dreams, are invitations to deeper obedience.

The dreamer and the visionary are kindred spirits — both called to believe what they've seen before the world sees it.

Wisdom Key: *Divine dreams and visions are not invitations to comfort—they are summons to surrender.*

What others meant to bury, God meant to build. The pit was not a prison; it was a passage. Every blow of rejection was shaping the shoulders that would one day carry responsibility.

What seemed like a setback was a setup, and every delay was divine design. God uses opposition as oxygen—it keeps the fire of purpose alive.

Joseph was not the only one who trembled beneath the weight of revelation. Every person who has ever heard God's whisper knows the ache that follows the promise.

You may not have a coat of many colors, but you have *carried questions, endured waiting,* and faced the sting of being *misunderstood.* Yet God wastes nothing—not even your delay. Every season of silence is shaping the vessel that will one day carry His answer.

Joseph's dream was no ordinary dream—it was God-given. And whenever God gives a dream or a vision, He often reveals the glory but conceals the grind.

The beauty of the calling is shown, but the burdens are hidden. The exaltation is prophesied, but not the pain that will precede it.

Nowhere in Joseph's dream did he see a *pit, slavery, prison,* or *betrayal.* Yet all of it was part of the process.

Why?

Because the dream had to be bigger than Joseph's comfort. It had to *mature* him, *break* him, and *shape* him into a vessel worthy of the assignment.

The path to the palace had to pass through trial so Joseph would be more than a ruler—he would become a redeemer.

Wisdom Key: *Every divine dream will provoke demonic attention and human opposition. Favor will always be followed by fire.*

Genesis 37 begins with a tension that many believers know all too well: *the weight of a dream you didn't ask for but can't deny.*

Joseph was only seventeen when God gave him a vision—one that would ignite *hatred* in his brothers, *disrupt* his family, and set in *motion* a journey that would change history.

The dream did not come through *study, fasting,* or *prayer.* It came by *divine initiation.* Joseph didn't seek the dream—the dream found him.

And that's how it often begins. God interrupts the ordinary with revelation. He inserts purpose into the unsuspecting heart.

But what Joseph didn't know—and what many of us fail to realize—is that the moment you receive a divine dream or vision, you become a target.

Joseph's dream revealed his future authority. His sheaf stood upright while others bowed. It was symbolic, prophetic, and undeniable.

Yet rather than being celebrated, it was met with hostility. His brothers couldn't handle the implications of what God was doing in Joseph.

And here's a truth worth noting: *sometimes the dream will offend those closest to you—not because of what you've done, but because of what God has spoken over you.*

The dream was never just about Joseph. It was about *preservation*. It was about *famine*. It was about *nations*.

Biblical commentators note that Joseph's dreams function not simply as personal revelations but as divine instruments that initiate a larger redemptive plan.

In the theological landscape of Genesis, dreams serve as vehicles of divine initiative—they are not given for entertainment or ego, but to reveal God's unfolding will in history.

The dream given to Joseph did more than elevate him—it activated a divine sequence of events that would preserve the covenant family through famine and fulfill God's promise to Abraham.

Spiritual Insight: *In God's economy, revelation is rarely isolated. It is communal, prophetic, and often disruptive to human plans.*

Joseph's dream was disruptive. It introduced *conflict, stirred jealousy, and broke the illusion of family peace.* But in breaking that illusion, it made room for *divine transformation.*

Joseph's youthful dream did not simply forecast rulership—it forecast the cost of becoming God's vessel. But the initial audience—his brothers— couldn't see past their own insecurity.

Jealousy blinded them to purpose. *Hatred* muted discernment. They plotted not against Joseph's character, but against his calling.

Not everyone will understand or accept the dream God gives you. In fact, the dream may isolate you from those you once walked closely with. Divine revelation has a way of setting you apart—not by your own choice, but by Spiritual necessity.

Your calling may demand that you walk alone before you're trusted to lead others. The misunderstanding you experience is not always personal—it is often prophetic. They plotted not against Joseph's character, but against his calling.

But let's consider this: *why would God give such a heavy dream to someone so young?*

Because God doesn't speak to your present maturity—He speaks to your future identity.

Joseph was not ready for Egypt, but he was chosen for Egypt. The dream was a seed that would grow in the soil of *adversity*. *Rejection* would water it. *Injustice* would fertilize it. And in time, God would bring it forth.

When God gives you a dream, He gives it with the end in mind. He sees past the pit, through the prison, and straight into the palace.

Joseph didn't understand it yet, but he was being drafted into a divine process. A process that would strip him of *immaturity*, break his *dependency on affirmation*, and *teach him to hear God above the noise.*

Every great assignment starts with a *dream*. But every dream must be *tested.*

The coat his father gave him may have marked him as favored, but it was the prison that made him a leader. The dreamer had to be developed. And for Joseph, that development began the moment God spoke.

Wisdom Key: *The dream is not a reward. It's a responsibility.*

Let God choose you. Let Him mature you. And don't despise the process that takes you from vision to fulfillment.

This is the beginning of your Joseph journey.

Reflective Questions:

1. How can you discern whether the dream or vision you carry was truly given by God and not shaped by personal ambition or emotion?

2. In what ways has divine favor in your life attracted friction, misunderstanding, or rejection—and what might God be developing in you through those experiences?

3. What does Joseph's journey reveal about the connection between revelation and refinement?

4. When God delays the fulfillment of your dream or vision, how can you remain faithful during seasons of silence and hiddenness?

5. What "coat" has God placed on your life—a mark of distinction or calling—and how are you stewarding it with humility and wisdom?

Reflection Summary: The Weight of a Dream

Every dream or vision given by God carries both a promise and a process. The same God who reveals destiny also refines character.

Like Joseph, we must learn that divine favor is not a shortcut to greatness but an invitation to endurance.

The pit, the prison, and *the palace* all serve one purpose—to prepare the dreamer and the visionary to handle the fulfillment without losing their faith.

Remember, what others meant to bury, God meant to build. Your waiting is not wasted.

Prayer

Lord, You are the Giver of dreams and the Revealer of visions. Thank You for trusting me with glimpses of Your plan.

Teach me to discern what is truly from You and to walk humbly through every season of testing.

When favor attracts fire, give me grace to stand. When delay feels discouraging, remind me that You are still working behind the scenes.

Refine me, shape me, and strengthen me until I become the vessel You can use for Your glory.

Let the dream You placed within me live on— pure, surrendered, and aligned with Your will.

In Jesus' name, Amen.

Chapter 2 — The Cost of the Coat

"They saw him afar off, even before he came near unto them, they conspired against him to slay him." — **Genesis 37:18**

Spiritual Principle

Divine favor will always draw the fire of human jealousy and spiritual resistance.

Joseph's coat was more than fabric—it was identity. It marked him as chosen and separated him from his brothers.

But the very thing that distinguished him also made him a target.

What was meant to cover him in love became a symbol of resentment.

The coat itself didn't provoke hatred—the combination of *the coat* and *the dream* was too much for his brothers to handle. **Favor** and **revelation** together can make you radiant to heaven but threatening to hell.

This is the cost of favor. Not everyone will celebrate what sets you apart, and not everyone close to you can handle what God is doing in your life.

God allowed Joseph to be sent by his father into the field—not to punish him, but to begin the process of divine separation.

The separation from his brothers was not just physical—it was prophetic. Joseph was not merely walking toward his brothers; *he was walking toward purpose, and that purpose required isolation.*

Spiritual Insight

There is always a cost to carrying something uncommon.

Separation in God's plan is never punishment—it is positioning. Before God entrusts you with visibility, He will enroll you in obscurity. The path to public favor always begins with private separation.

Joseph's journey teaches us that betrayal is not always personal—it is often prophetic.

Though it appeared as betrayal, it was God's hand moving behind the scenes. Each painful moment—being thrown into the pit, sold to the Ishmaelites, falsely accused in Potiphar's house, and forgotten in prison—was divinely timed and intentionally allowed.

These weren't just trials; they were training grounds. God wasn't merely testing Joseph's faith—He was forming Joseph's future.

When people don't understand your calling, they'll fight what they cannot define. His brothers hated what Joseph represented: *God's favor, God's voice,* and *God's authority.* Yet in their attempt to destroy him, they positioned him.

The pit was not the end—it was a passage. God used their cruelty to relocate Joseph from comfort to calling.

Theology of Divine Providence

From a theological perspective, **Genesis 37** reveals the mystery of divine providence. God's silence in the midst of betrayal is not absence—it is orchestration.

As the **New Interpreter's Bible** notes, *"The invisibility of God does not mean the inactivity of God."*

Even as Joseph was stripped, thrown, and sold, God was moving—quietly, deliberately, and purposefully.

The text says nothing of Joseph *resisting*. He doesn't *argue* or *cry out.* This silence is not weakness—*it is surrender,* a sign of early spiritual maturity. He is being formed inwardly for an outward purpose.

What we wear externally can be taken. But what God deposits in our spirit cannot be removed by the hands of men.

Biblical Reflection

When the brothers stripped Joseph of his coat, they removed the outward sign of favor—but they could not strip the dream.

The promise remained intact, buried in his soul, guarded by the hand of God.

Every leader, every servant of God, must pass through seasons where you are *misunderstood, mistreated,* and *mishandled*—not because you've done wrong, but because God is making you right.

Theological Truth: Before God elevates a man, He separates him. Before He trusts him with power, He trains him with pressure.

Parallel Truths

David's anointing drew Saul's spear. **Esther's** crown drew Haman's plot. **Mary's** womb drew Herod's wrath.

Every mantle carries warfare, and every favor invites fire.

This is the spiritual law of distinction: *the greater the call, the greater the cost.*

So, when favor begins to stir resistance around you, don't panic—*prepare.* The opposition confirms that something divine is taking shape.

Wisdom Keys

- Favor will always reveal both your friends and your foes.

- If your calling never costs you, it may not be from God.

- The pit is not your grave—it's your gateway.

- Divine separation precedes divine elevation.

- What looks like rejection may actually be God's redirection.

Deeper Study — Genesis 37: 18–36

Observation — What Do We See?

The story opens not with conversation but with distance: *"They saw him afar off."*

Every verb that follows—*saw, conspired, stripped, cast, sold*—marks movement away from safety and toward surrender. Hidden in those motions is divine direction.

We see:

- The coat – a visible emblem of favor that both identifies and isolates.

- The brothers' eyes – sight ruled by jealousy; envy distorts perception.

- The pit – the place of descent where vision meets reality.

- Silence – no words from Joseph, no voice from heaven, yet heaven is still at work.

Favor, distance, and silence create the atmosphere where God's unseen purpose begins to unfold.

Interpretation — What Did It Mean Then?

For ancient readers, this scene showed more than sibling rivalry—it displayed **covenant movement.**

Through a jealous act, God began positioning Joseph to preserve a people.

The stripping of the coat symbolized the transfer from human honor to divine purpose.

In Hebrew culture, garments marked inheritance and rank.

By losing the coat, Joseph gained something greater: the training of his soul.

The pit became the womb of destiny where pride died and faith was born.

Commentary Insight — Favoritism, Jealousy, and Providence

Genesis 37 also reveals how human favoritism and divine providence often intersect.

Jacob's gift of the coat of many colors exposed his favoritism toward Joseph—a father's affection that stirred jealousy among the brothers.

Yet even that favoritism was woven into God's plan. The coat pointed beyond a parent's preference; it foreshadowed Joseph's future authority and royal destiny.

The garment that marked him as special in his father's house would one day be mirrored by the robe of rulership in Pharaoh's palace.

What began as favoritism became a prophetic symbol of the calling Joseph would one day carry.

The brothers' envy set the process of destiny in motion. Their hatred led to betrayal, but God turned betrayal into a bridge.

Through the chaos of family conflict, the unseen hand of providence was at work.

This reminds us that even when life feels unfair or relationships turn sour, God uses difficulty as development. He transforms rejection into refinement and pain into purpose. Nothing in Joseph's story was wasted—and nothing in ours will be either.

Word Study: Providence

Providence is **the wise and purposeful care of God** by which He directs all things—both seen and unseen—toward the fulfillment of His divine will.

It means that **God is never absent, never passive, and never surprised.**

Through His providence, He works in all circumstances (good or bad) and through all people (faithful or flawed) to accomplish what He has already ordained.

In simpler terms:

Providence is **God's hand in the details,** turning what seems random or unfair into part of His redemptive plan.

Biblical Examples of Providence

- **Joseph** — God used betrayal, slavery, and imprisonment to place him in a position to save a nation (Genesis 45:7–8).

- **Esther** — God arranged her rise to royalty "for such a time as this" (Esther 4:14).

- **Ruth** — God guided her steps from famine and loss to the lineage of Christ.

- **Jesus** — Even the cross, the greatest act of injustice, became the stage for salvation.

Providence is the invisible thread of God's will, weaving every trial, every delay, and every betrayal into a design that reveals His glory and secures His purpose.

Scriptural Echoes:

- **Genesis 45:7–8** — *"God sent me before you to preserve life."*

- **Romans 8:28** — *"All things work together for good to them that love God."*

- **Esther 4:14** — *"Who knoweth whether thou art come to the kingdom for such a time as this?"*

Theological Principles

1. **Providence Works in the Shadows**.
   God's silence is strategy, not absence.

2. **Favor Requires Formation.** The chosen
   must first be changed.

3. **Separation Is Sacred Preparation.**
   Isolation is the hallway to elevation.

4. **Descent Precedes Dominion.** Every
   crown is forged in a crucible.

Wisdom Key: What man strips, God restores—
and He restores it with greater authority.

Application — What Does It Mean for Us Today?

- When favor brings friction, remember: resistance is often recognition.

- When God is silent, stay faithful—He's still scripting your story.

- When you're stripped of visible blessings, hold to invisible grace.

- When you feel buried, trust that you've been planted.

Ask Yourself:

- What "coat" has God allowed to be removed so that I can be refined?

- Can I see my separation as sacred, not spiteful?

- Will I let the pit make me bitter—or make me better?

Prayer Thought

Lord, refine my response more than my reputation.

Use every stripping to strengthen my surrender.

Summary Thought

Genesis 37 reminds us that divine purpose often enters through human pain.

The hands that hurt you may be the very instruments God uses to lift you.

The pit is temporary, but the plan is eternal.

Stay still. Stay surrendered.

The cost of the coat is the price of the call.

Reflective Questions:

1. What outward signs of favor in your life have made you a target of misunderstanding or jealousy?

2. How has God used betrayal or separation in your past to redirect you toward your purpose?

3. Are there areas where you've confused divine preparation with punishment?

4. In what ways have you seen God's silent providence working behind the scenes?

5. What spiritual qualities do you think God is forming in you during your current trials?

Reflective Summary:

Chapter 2 confronts us with a truth many avoid: favor comes with a cost.

Joseph's coat was not only a symbol of love—it was a spiritual identifier marking him for both promotion and persecution.

His betrayal was not an accident—it was divine arrangement.

God used the very ones who hated Joseph to push him into destiny.

The pit was not the end; it was the passage.

In seasons of stripping, silence, and misunderstanding, God remains sovereign.

If we allow Him, He will use every wound to refine us, every betrayal to reposition us, and every loss to prepare us for leadership.

The same God who allows the stripping also ordains the stitching.

What was torn in the pit will be tailored for the palace.

This is the cost of the coat—and the shaping of the called.

Prayer:

Father, thank You for the favor You've placed on my life. Even when I don't understand the pain that comes with it, help me to trust Your plan.

Teach me to embrace the pit as preparation, not punishment.

Separate me from what distracts me from Your purpose. Form in me a spirit of surrender and patience.

I choose to see betrayal as redirection and silence as sacred training.

May I never value the coat more than the call, and may I walk through every trial with faith in Your promise.

In Jesus' name, Amen.

Chapter 3 — Sent, but Sold

"Then there passed by Midianite merchantmen; and they drew and lifted up Joseph out of the pit, and sold Joseph to the Ishmaelites for twenty pieces of silver: and they brought Joseph into Egypt."

— Genesis 37:28

Spiritual Principle

Before God can use you publicly, He must first break you privately.

Joseph was not just sold by his brothers—he was **sent by God.** The transaction that looked like tragedy was, in truth, a **transfer of destiny.**

69

The caravan carrying him away was not a vehicle of loss but a **chariot of purpose.**

When God ordains your future, even betrayal becomes transportation. This is the mystery of divine sending: the pit may be deep, but it is never purposeless.

Spiritual Insight — The Mystery of the Broken Seed

Jesus revealed the pattern of all spiritual fruitfulness:

"Except a corn of wheat fall into the ground and die, it abideth alone: but if it die, it bringeth forth much fruit." — **John 12:24**

Every great work of God begins with a **burial.** Joseph's pit was his **planting ground.** The soil that seemed to swallow him was the very ground from which his destiny would sprout.

Like the seed, Joseph had to be **buried before he could bloom.** Hiddenness is heaven's way of preparing harvest.

When you find yourself covered in darkness, remember—**God plants what He intends to raise.**

The Breaking of the Outer Man — Watchman Nee's Wisdom

The Chinese teacher **Watchman Nee** described this mystery as *"the breaking of the outer man."* The outer man—*our pride, emotion, and self-reliance*—must be shattered so the inner life of the Spirit can flow freely.

Joseph's colorful coat was not his only covering. He still wore the garments of youthful arrogance, favoritism, and untested ambition. Before he could wear Pharaoh's robe of authority, he had to lose his father's robe of affection.

God allowed him to be ***misunderstood, stripped, and confined*** so that his spirit could be refined.

As **Watchman Nee** wrote, paraphrased:

"God must bring us to the end of our own strength so that His life may flow unhindered through us."

Even Jesus Himself modeled this breaking in **Gethsemane**—where the will of man bowed to the will of God. Submission always precedes manifestation.

The Theology of the Pit — Burial Before Resurrection

The pit represents that sacred place where God kills what hinders and awakens what helps.

It is the **grave of self-dependence** and the **womb of divine dependence.**

- Joseph in the pit — death of comfort.

- Jesus in the tomb — death of self-will.

- The believer in testing — death of independence.

The pit is never the end of the story—it is where resurrection begins.

Before God raises a man, He first allows him to descend—so that glory belongs to God alone.

Deeper Study — Genesis 37: 23–36

Observation — What Do We See?

In this scene, betrayal becomes business.

His brothers strip, conspire, and sell—yet every movement fulfills heaven's unseen timetable.

We see:

- **Betrayal** — Jealousy dressed as justice.

- **Blood** — The mark of false evidence.

- **Business** — Twenty pieces of silver, the price of a slave.

- **Boundaries** — Joseph crosses from promise to process.

Heaven is silent—but not absent. The Lord of providence is orchestrating redemption through human rebellion.

Interpretation — What Did It Mean Then?

To ancient readers, Joseph's sale would have echoed the voice of **divine irony:** the favored son rejected by his brethren becomes the savior of the same family.

God was already arranging Egypt's storehouse before famine ever arrived.

What looked like tragedy was **transportation;** what felt like rejection was **relocation.** The pit was the **portal.**

Joseph's descent was the first step toward Israel's deliverance.

Commentary Insight — The Seed and the Soul

Jesus' teaching in **John 12:24** reveals a universal law of the Spirit: **life only flows through death.** Joseph's story embodies that law.

Each time he was lowered—*into a pit, into slavery, into prison*—he was being sown deeper into God's purpose.

Like a seed, he carried potential that could only be released through **breaking.** God allowed circumstances to crush the shell of pride so the life of humility could emerge. True leadership is born not from giftedness but from **brokenness.**

God buries His treasures before He reveals them.

Providence in the Paradox — Sent, but Sold

Genesis 37 tells the story from the ground—
betrayal and envy. **Psalm 105:17** retells it from
the heavens:

*"He sent a man before them, even Joseph, who
was sold for a servant."*

At first glance, the two seem to disagree—was
Joseph **sold** or **sent?**

The answer is both.

The Hebrew verb for *"sent"* also means
appointed or commissioned.

What men meant for harm, God meant for help.

While his brothers sold him in hatred, God sent him in purpose.

- Genesis reveals man's motive—**sin.**

- Psalms reveal God's motive—**salvation.**

The same event carries two dimensions: earth's betrayal and heaven's commission. **Psalm 105** doesn't rewrite Genesis; it **reframes** it from God's perspective.

Joseph's sale was not divine punishment but divine placement.

Even wickedness was woven into providence.

God's sovereignty does not erase human guilt,
yet human sin cannot obstruct divine will.
Heaven used human hands to forward holy plans.

Joseph wasn't merely sold—he was **sent.** And
what seemed like rejection became the road to
redemption.

When God's Sending Doesn't Look Like Sending

Oftentimes, God's sending does not look the way we expect it to look.

His assignments rarely come dressed in glory; they come wrapped in *humility, hardship,* and *hiddenness.*

Look at **Jesus**—sent to save the world, yet *born in a manger, misunderstood by men,* and *crucified between thieves.*

His greatest victory wore the disguise of defeat.

Consider **the manna**—heaven's bread that looked like flakes of dew.

It did not resemble abundance, yet it sustained a nation.

Think of **David**—anointed king, but sent back to tend sheep until the battlefield called his name. The oil was on him long before the crown was.

And remember **John the Baptist**—a man sent from God whose pulpit was the wilderness, whose clothing was rough, whose diet was wild, and whose ministry ended behind prison walls.

Yet Jesus called him the greatest ever born of a woman.

Every one of these lives teaches that divine sending often comes through **unfamiliar roads**—through the desert, the dungeon, or the cross.

God's call may lead us into obscurity before it brings us into influence.

His path may strip before it crowns, bury before it raises, break before it blesses.

But in each case, the sending is sovereign.

What looks like setback is strategy; what feels like rejection is redirection.

The true mark of being sent is not comfort but **commission**—and God's purpose, not man's perception, defines success.

Word Study — Brokenness (Greek: suntribō)

Meaning: to crush, shatter, or break in pieces; to make useful again through breaking.

Used of pottery in the ancient world that, once shattered, could be remade into finer vessels.

In God's kingdom, brokenness is never waste—it's refinement.

Every crushing release something sacred.

- Joseph's breaking released wisdom.

- Jesus' breaking released salvation.

- Our breaking releases glory.

Theological Principles

- **Burial Precedes Breakthrough.** What looks like an ending is often an entrance.

- **Brokenness Releases Life.** The shell must crack for the Spirit to flow.

- **Providence Overrides Plotting**. God's plan stands even when people scheme.

- **Obedience After Offense.** God's servants must bless those who betrayed them.

Wisdom Key: *The same hands that push you down may unknowingly be pushing you into purpose.*

Application — What Does It Mean for Us Today?

If you've been betrayed, don't only see the **seller**—see the **Sender.**

When you feel buried, remember: **seeds are buried too— not dead but destined.**

When you face breaking, know that God is releasing something greater inside you.

Accept the pit as **preparation,** not punishment.

Ask Yourself:

1. What part of me still resists being broken?

2. Can I see God's hand in the very thing that hurt me?

3. Am I willing to be hidden until His timing reveals me?

Prayer Thought

Lord, help me to see purpose in my pain.

Teach me to embrace the burial so that new life can spring forth.

Let my breaking become someone else's blessing.

Summary Thought

The paradox of Joseph's life—and of ours—is this:

Man sold him, but God sent him.

The same pit that buried his pride birthed his power.

Every breaking became a blessing in disguise.

The outer shell was crushed, but the seed lived on—and multiplied.

This is the gospel written in Genesis: death before resurrection, breaking before blessing.

Reflective Questions:

1. How has God used the actions of others to redirect your life toward His purpose?

2. What area of your life is God asking you to surrender so that His life can flow freely?

3. Can you identify a season when being "sold" was really God's way of sending you?

4. In what ways has brokenness deepened your faith?

5. What fruit has come from your seasons of hiddenness and pain?

Reflective Summary — The Power of the Broken Seed

Chapter 3 teaches that God's sending often hides inside man's selling.

The pit and the caravan were instruments of providence.

The breaking of the seed released the life of the Spirit.

Just as Jesus' body was broken to bring forth eternal life, Joseph's brokenness preserved nations.

Every believer who bears fruit must pass through the same pattern—*planted, pressed,* and *raised.*

Brokenness is not defeat; it is divine design.

The pit is the proving ground of purpose.

Prayer:

Father, thank You for the mercy of Your providence.

When others sell me short, You send me forward.

When I am broken, You are releasing something greater within me.

Teach me to welcome the breaking that brings forth Your life.

Crush pride, silence complaint, and *strengthen surrender.*

May every wound become a well of wisdom, and may my life, like Joseph's and like Christ's, feed many in their famine.

In Jesus' name, Amen.

Wisdom Keys

- God's sending often travels under the passport of pain.

- The wilderness is not rejection—it is redirection.

- The pit may hide you, but it cannot halt you.

- What God buries, He intends to raise.

- True promotion begins where self-reliance ends.

Chapter 4 — The House That Tested Him

"And Joseph was brought down to Egypt; and Potiphar, an officer of Pharaoh, captain of the guard, an Egyptian, bought him of the hands of the Ishmaelites..." — **Genesis 39:1**

Spiritual Principle

Before God gives you the palace, He will prove you in the house.

Can you imagine what it was like for Joseph to be abused and misused by his own brothers—those he grew up with, those who should have loved and protected him?

Instead, they tore from him the coat of favor and sold him into the hands of passing strangers.

The Ishmaelites and Midianite travelers were not friends—they were slave traders. To be taken from all that is familiar and loved, and delivered into bondage and forced labor, would have broken the spirit of most men.

But Joseph was not most men. While his body was sold into slavery, his dream remained free. God had already marked him for something greater, and though he was betrayed, stripped, and trafficked, heaven still had the final word.

Joseph's journey now takes him to Potiphar's house—a place that, at first glance, appears to be a step up from the pit. He's no longer in danger of death.

He's clothed again. He has a roof over his head.
But make no mistake: this house will test him
more deeply than the pit ever could.

The pit reveals your pain.
But the house reveals your heart.

Transitional Insight — From the Pit to the House

Every new season comes with a new examination.

The pit tested Joseph's *faith in isolation*; the house tested his *faithfulness in opportunity*.

- In the pit, he learned to trust God when he had nothing.

- In the house, he learned to honor God when he had everything.

The same God who watched him cry in the darkness of the pit was now watching him work in the brightness of prosperity. God doesn't just test us in loss—He tests us in leadership.

The pit crushed his pride; the house refined his integrity.

And in both places, the Lord was with him.

Observation — What Do We See?

In **Genesis 39** we witness the rhythm of divine consistency: *"The Lord was with Joseph."* That phrase appears four times **(vv. 2, 3, 21, 23),** anchoring Joseph's success not in his surroundings but in his Source.

Every shift of circumstance—pit, house, prison—was accompanied by the same statement: **the presence of God remained constant.**

We see:

- **Progress:** Joseph moves from servant to overseer.

- **Purity:** He refuses the advances of Potiphar's wife.

- **Persecution:** He suffers unjustly for doing right.

- **Providence:** God turns every setback into setup.

What seems like contradiction is confirmation— Joseph's faithfulness in obscurity kept him under divine supervision.

Wisdom Key: When the presence of God is with you, the place you're in can't limit what God will do.

Translation Insight — Layers of Meaning Across Versions

- **Verse 2: KJV** calls Joseph a "prosperous man," but **NIV** and **ESV** say *"so that he prospered"* or *"became successful."* **The Amplified** adds, *"even though a slave."* → Prosperity in God's eyes is not possession but presence.

- **Verse 3:** All versions agree that Potiphar *saw* the Lord was with Joseph. → Divine favor is visible, not just felt.

- **Verse 5:** *"The Lord blessed the Egyptian's house for Joseph's sake."* **(KJV)** → **One righteous life can shift an entire environment.**

- **Verse 6**: *"Goodly and well favoured"* **(KJV)** is rendered *"well-built and handsome"* **(NIV).** → Joseph's physical beauty became a battleground for his integrity.

- **Verse 9: NLT** adds relational tone — *"How could I violate his trust and sin against God?"* → **Sin is not just disobedience—it's betrayal of divine relationship.**

- **Verse 21: ESV** renders *"mercy"* as *"steadfast love (ḥesed),"* revealing that God's favor was **covenantal,** not conditional.

- **Verse 23:** The chapter begins and ends with *"The Lord was with Joseph."* → His location changed, but God's presence did not.

Hebrew Note: The phrase *"The Lord was with Joseph"* uses the covenant name **YHWH**— signifying *personal, relational presence, not general blessing.* Success was the consequence of companionship, not the cause of it.

The Test of Stewardship

Joseph was no longer wearing his father's coat. He was wearing **a servant's robe**—but he wore it with excellence. He did not wait for a better situation to serve God faithfully. He served where he was planted.

Wisdom Key: What you do with little will determine what God trusts you with next.

Joseph mastered the art of being faithful in limitation. He didn't let bitterness hinder his excellence. He didn't use injustice as an excuse to slack. He managed another man's house with the same diligence he would later bring to Pharaoh's court.

This is divine stewardship in action—proving capable with what belongs to another.

Christ Connection — Servanthood Before Sovereignty

Even Jesus, the Son of God, did not bypass servanthood on His way to kingship.

- He washed feet before He wore a crown.

- He submitted to a carpenter's house before commanding heaven's host.

Likewise, Joseph's greatness was not proven in Pharaoh's court—it was forged in Potiphar's kitchen.

Divine promotion is always preceded by divine proving.

Wisdom Key: If you cannot serve under authority, you are not ready to carry authority.

The Test of Character

Joseph was God-conscious. He lived with an awareness that every action he took was seen by the Almighty.

Even in Egypt, far removed from his father's house and the spiritual heritage he was raised under, he never lost sight of God.

His decisions weren't based on circumstance or convenience—they were rooted in **conviction.**

While others might have compromised for comfort or survival, Joseph feared the Lord more than he feared the consequences of integrity.

His conscience was not seared by pain, nor dulled by bitterness. Instead, it remained alive and sensitive, tethered to a moral compass aligned with heaven.

When in the process of divine breaking and character building, *a person often goes from one breaking moment to the next—with little to no time to recover.* **This was Joseph's reality.**

No sooner had he found favor in Potiphar's house than he was thrust into another storm of false accusation and unjust punishment.

God was not punishing Joseph—He was preparing him. Each trial chipped away at the outer man so the inner strength, molded by God's hand, could emerge. It's a painful process, but a necessary one for those called to carry weighty assignments.

Then came the greater test—Potiphar's wife. When temptation enters the room, character is revealed. Joseph was handsome. He was trusted. He was alone. And yet, he **resisted.**

Not because he feared Potiphar—but because he feared God.

"How then can I do this great wickedness, and sin against God?" — **Genesis 39:9**

Joseph's integrity was not situational—it was spiritual. He understood that sin was not just a betrayal of man, but a violation against God.

The War Within — The Battle of the Anointed

Every anointed person faces this crossroads: will I protect my calling or please my craving?

- Samson had strength but no restraint, and it cost him his sight.

- David had anointing but let desire overtake discernment, and it cost him peace.

- Joseph, though young and handsome, chose restraint over release.

He conquered not by fighting sin but by fleeing it. True holiness is not found in proximity to temptation but in separation from it.

Wisdom Key: What you refuse to entertain today will not have power to enslave you tomorrow.

Watchman Insight

Watchman Nee wrote that *"God often permits false accusation to crucify the outer man so that the life of the Spirit may be revealed."*

Joseph was accused of the very thing he fled from. Potiphar's wife lied. Joseph was cast into prison.

It seemed unjust—but it was divine.

Spiritual Reality: Sometimes obedience lands you in darker places—but those are often the places of deeper preparation.

Interpretation — What Did It Mean Then?

In Joseph's time, to be a Hebrew slave in an Egyptian officer's house was the lowest social position imaginable—yet God's presence reversed the order of the house.

Potiphar's estate prospered because a covenant man served there.

This fulfills a divine principle seen throughout Scripture: *wherever God's people dwell, His blessing follows* **(Genesis 30:27; Deuteronomy 28:8).**

Joseph's story mirrors Israel's story in miniature—favored, oppressed, yet preserved through obedience.

The text reveals that holiness in private always precedes influence in public.

Even when stripped of power, Joseph retained presence, and presence produced prosperity.

God was training him not only to lead Egypt's storehouses, but to steward heaven's presence among pagan power.

Translation Note: ESV's rendering "steadfast love" for "mercy" **(v. 21)** translates the Hebrew ḥesed—covenant love. God's faithfulness to Joseph was not sentimental; it was relational and unbreakable.

Commentary Reflection

The **New Interpreter's Bible** notes the rhythm of Joseph's life: *favor, fall, favor, fall.*

Through every descent, God was carving out a vessel of *purity, patience,* and *power.*

The house was the testing ground. And Joseph emerged approved.

- He was betrayed, but he didn't break.

- He was tempted, but he didn't yield.

- He was lied on, but he remained faithful.

Theological Principles

1. **Divine Presence > Position.** God's favor rests on character, not circumstance.

2. **Integrity Is the Currency of Promotion.** Heaven entrusts influence to those faithful in obscurity.

3. **Temptation Is a Test of Worship.** Sin is misplaced devotion before it is moral failure.

4. **Righteous Suffering Is Redemptive.** The unjust suffering of God's servants advances His saving plan **(1 Peter 2:19-23).**

5. **Faithfulness Is Measured by Stewardship.** How we handle another's house determines how God entrusts us with our own.

Application Insight — The House Tests of Today

Every believer will face a Potiphar's house— a place where faithfulness is measured not by applause, but by obedience.

Your *"house"* might be *your workplace, your ministry, your marriage,* or *even a season of silence where God watches how you handle what belongs to another.*

- Do you cut corners when no one's watching?

- Do you stay humble when promoted?

- Do you resist temptation when opportunity presents itself?

Before God releases you into your own vision, He will observe how you handle someone else's.

Before He trusts you with a platform, He'll see how you respond in private.

The house reveals what kind of heart you'll have in the palace.

Application — What Does It Mean for Us Today?

Every believer must graduate from the *house test.* It is one thing to pray for a platform—it is another to pass the proving ground of private obedience.

- When assigned tasks beneath your title— serve with excellence.

- When opportunity to sin appears harmless—remember Joseph's reverence.

- When misunderstood—remain consistent.

- When falsely accused—trust God's vindication rather than man's validation.

The Potiphar's house seasons expose whether you're serving for attention or out of affection for God.

It's in these quiet seasons that spiritual maturity is formed.

Wisdom Key: The way you serve in secret determines how God will use you in public.

Wisdom Summary

Before God gives you a platform, He will give
you a proving place.

Potiphar's house was not the palace—but it
prepared Joseph to rule one.

It was the house that tested him—and the fire
that forged him.

Reflective Questions:

1. In what ways has your current environment become a testing ground for your character and calling?

2. Are you serving with excellence even in a place that feels beneath your potential?

3. How do you respond when no one sees your faithfulness but God?

4. What temptations in your life are challenging your integrity, and how are you confronting them?

5. Can you trust God's process when doing the right thing leads to suffering or misunderstanding?

Reflective Summary:

Potiphar's house teaches us that the tests of life are rarely loud. They come in the quiet moments of stewardship, the hidden battles of integrity, and the daily decisions of faithfulness.

Joseph didn't need the spotlight to prove he was chosen—he needed the shadows to become mature.

Promotion doesn't begin in the palace—it begins in the places where no one claps.
The house tested Joseph's will, his heart, and his holiness.

Though the test ended

Prayer:

Lord,

Thank You for the hidden places. Thank You for the houses that refine and for the tests that reveal.

Teach me to serve with joy, to resist with courage, and to trust You when no one else understands.

Help me to remain faithful even when falsely accused or forgotten. Let my integrity speak louder than my words, and let my obedience be my worship.

Mold me into a vessel that honors You in private as well as in public. I receive the fire of refinement, knowing You are preparing me for greater things.

In Jesus' name, Amen.

Chapter 5 — When Obedience Feels Like Rejection

"And Joseph's master took him, and put him into the prison, a place where the king's prisoners were bound: and he was there in the prison. But the Lord was with Joseph, and shewed him mercy, and gave him favour in the sight of the keeper of the prison."

— Genesis 39:20–21

Spiritual Principle

Sometimes the path of obedience will lead you through the valley of rejection —but it is still the path of God.

Joseph obeyed God in Potiphar's house, resisted temptation, and chose righteousness over reward.

Yet instead of being honored for his *integrity,* he was *falsely accused, stripped again,* and *thrown into another dark place.*

From the pit to Potiphar's house to prison—the pattern seemed to repeat.

Faithfulness did not bring immediate reward; it brought another round of rejection.

Many assume obedience should lead straight to blessing, but in God's training ground, obedience often leads first to **breaking.**

The pit tested his *endurance.* The house tested his *integrity.*

Now the prison would test his trust in God's purpose.

Observation — What Do We See?

Genesis 39:20–23 reveals a divine paradox: the faithful man is bound, but the Lord remains with him.

Repeatedly the text declares, *"The Lord was with Joseph."*

Even in the dungeon, the same presence that prospered him in the house abided with him in the cell.

We see:

- **Injustice without intervention** — Joseph is punished for righteousness.

- **Isolation with intimacy** — The Lord's presence meets him in confinement.

- **Favor in the furnace** — Divine favor follows him even behind bars.

- **Steadfast mercy** — God's covenant love (ḥesed) sustains him.

The chapter closes as it began—with the presence of God as the final word over every circumstance.

Wisdom Key: Even when obedience costs you, the presence of God keeps you.

Translation Insights — Genesis 39:20–23

Version	Rendering
KJV	"The Lord … shewed him mercy."
ESV	"The Lord … showed him steadfast love."
NIV	"The Lord … showed him kindness."
CSB	"The Lord … extended kindness to him."
AMP	"The Lord … showed him lovingkindness and favor."

The Hebrew term **ḥesed** means faithful, loyal, enduring love.

It is not sentimental pity but covenant commitment.

Even though Joseph was locked away by man, he was embraced by mercy from God.

His chains could not cancel the covenant.

Insight: The Lord's presence is not proven by open doors but by unbreakable love.

Interpretation — What Did It Mean Then?

In ancient Egypt, imprisonment under royal authority was indefinite and without appeal.

A Hebrew slave accused of assaulting his master's wife would have faced execution.

That Joseph's life was spared already signals divine intervention.

The Lord's steadfast love in the prison was not deliverance from the situation, but endurance within it.

This was **preparation, not punishment.**

What looked like *demotion* was *direction*—each step downward carried Joseph closer to destiny.

His dungeon adjoined Pharaoh's court; the road to the throne passed through the cell.

Like Christ, Joseph's righteousness led to rejection, his integrity to isolation, and his obedience to opposition.

Yet both were **sent, not sentenced.**

Parallel Insight:

- Moses was driven from Egypt before returning as deliverer.

- Jeremiah was imprisoned for prophesying truth.

- Daniel was thrown into a lion's den for his devotion.

- John the Baptist was beheaded for confronting sin.

- Christ was crucified for obedience to the Father's will.

In every case, divine purpose prevailed through human injustice.

Theological Principles

1. **Obedience Is Not a Guarantee of Immediate Reward.** Doing right may bring rejection before reward **(1 Peter 2:19-21).**

2. **God's Presence Transforms Every Place**. When the Lord is with you, even a prison becomes a sanctuary **(Psalm 139:7-10).**

3. **Covenant Love Is Stronger Than Circumstance.** The ḥesed of God remains constant when conditions change.

4. **Preparation Precedes Promotion.** The Lord uses confinement to prepare for stewardship.

5. **Faithfulness Under Fire Is Heaven's Credential.** What we endure in obscurity determines what we can carry in visibility.

Spiritual Insight — The Silent Season

The prison was more than punishment—it symbolized the silent season between promise and fulfillment.

No dreams. No applause. No explanation. Only waiting.

This is where many lose heart. *We obey, yet doors close. We pray, yet silence answers.*

But in heaven's process, silence is not absence— it is **shaping.**

The dungeon of delay refines us in ways success never could.

Joseph's waiting was not wasted time—it was **weighing time.**

God was measuring him for the mantle he would soon carry.

Wisdom Key: God hides you before He hands you influence.

Joseph's Imprisonment — A Heavenly Assignment

Joseph's imprisonment was not just an earthly sentence—it was a heavenly assignment.

The dungeon became a deeper place of surrender where the applause of Potiphar's house faded and the silence of misunderstanding took hold.

Yet it was in that silence that God was closest.

He stripped Joseph of any reliance on people, position, or recognition. He was now truly alone with God.

In this isolation, Joseph's obedience reached its purest expression—not before an audience, but in the hidden chambers of confinement.

Leadership in God's Kingdom begins where reputation ends. The world saw a prison; God saw a proving ground.

There, Joseph's spiritual muscles strengthened. He learned to interpret dreams not for advantage but to serve others.

He discovered that influence flows from humility, and that elevation comes through enduring hardship without offense.

Watchman Nee taught that *"the breaking of the outer man is the beginning of spiritual ministry."*

Joseph's gifting was never the problem; his anointing was evident.

But the vessel that carried the gift had to be shattered and shaped into something holy.

This is what separates **charisma from calling**— what distinguishes **popularity from purpose.**

Even in prison, Joseph found favor.

The keeper entrusted him with responsibility because **the Lord was with him.** God's presence is not limited by walls or chains.

The favor of God flows not to those who strive, but to those who submit.

Obedience, even when it leads to rejection, is never wasted.

It tests, forms, and eventually distinguishes the true leader from the false.

Joseph's rejection was not a setback—it was a setup.

Not only for a throne in Egypt, but for a legacy of redemption.

Commentary Reflection

The **New Interpreter's Bible** notes Joseph's rhythm of *"favor and fall"* is not failure but formation.

God's favor does not prevent trials—it accompanies us through them.

Each descent chisels away what cannot enter destiny.

When obedience lands us in rejection, it reveals whether we serve God for reward or for relationship.

The furnace of faith proves what flatter seasons conceal.

Joseph's righteousness cost him everything—but also **qualified** him for everything God had planned.

The prison became the final classroom before his promotion.

Application — What Does It Mean for Us Today?

If you've ever done right and suffered wrong, you're in good company. The righteous path often winds through dark corridors.

Your obedience may cost you friendship, reputation, or opportunity—but it will never cost you God's favor.

The same Lord who was with Joseph in Potiphar's house walked with him into the prison.

Modern Parallels:

- The believer who refuses compromise may lose a job but gain character.

- The servant who stays faithful in silence may lose visibility but gain spiritual authority.

- The disciple who stands for truth may lose support but gain divine approval.

Obedience is never wasted—it is *recorded, refined,* and *rewarded* in God's timing.

Wisdom Key: When obedience leads to rejection, it proves your loyalty is to God, not applause.

Observation of Providence — From Rejection to Repositioning

Even the prison was positioned by providence.

The royal dungeon lay near Pharaoh's residence—where the king's cupbearer and baker were confined.

God placed Joseph in proximity to his next divine connection.

The same rejection that seemed to ruin him repositioned him for revelation.

Every closed door was a divine detour toward the throne.

Note:

KJV — *"The Lord made it to prosper."*

ESV — *"Whatever he did, the Lord made it succeed."*

NIV — *"The Lord gave him success in whatever he did."*

Each emphasizes divine agency—Joseph's success was **Spirit-made, not self-made.**

Wisdom Key: The Lord's presence doesn't merely accompany you—it accelerates divine purpose even in confinement.

Reflective Questions:

1. Have you ever obeyed God and found yourself misunderstood or rejected because of it?

2. What areas of your life might be undergoing divine breaking rather than punishment?

3. How may God be shaping your character in isolation?

4. How can you serve others—even in confinement or obscurity?

5. Can you trust that rejection might be divine redirection?

Reflective Summary — Obedience in the Dark

Joseph's prison season shows that God's path to promotion often passes through pain. The *silence, betrayal,* and *rejection* are not signs of abandonment but of refinement.

Joseph didn't lose his dream in the dungeon—he grew into it. The prison refined his motives, deepened his gift, and enlarged his capacity to lead.

In a world that celebrates visibility, God builds His leaders in *secrecy.* If obedience has led you into what feels like rejection—remember Joseph.

The pit didn't cancel the promise; the prison didn't derail the plan. Both were part of God's process.

The place of confinement became the platform of preparation. There Joseph learned to *manage complexity, interpret vision,* and *endure waiting without answers.*

He remained faithful though forgotten—a mark of spiritual maturity. Obedience does not guarantee immediate reward. Sometimes obeying God costs everything before it brings anything.

Yet the God who sees in secret rewards openly.

The same dungeon where Joseph was forgotten became the place where he was remembered and raised.

Divine rejection is not abandonment—it is alignment.

Lesson: Don't rush out of the dungeon. Don't curse your confinement. It is in this hidden, broken, misunderstood place that God does His best work.

Like Joseph, we rarely recognize God's hand while it's shaping us. He didn't see a throne ahead; he only longed for relief.

But God had greater intentions: not just deliverance, but dominion—not survival, but stewardship. When we pray for escape, God works for transformation.

The *injustice, betrayal,* and *false accusations* were chisels in the Master's hand, crafting a vessel fit for national provision.

Even when unseen or unfelt, God is forming something eternal in us.

Prophetic Summary:

The prison was not punishment—it was preparation. Before Joseph could interpret dreams for others, he had to live through his own delay.

His obedience cost him freedom but gained him favor. He was misunderstood yet molded; confined yet connected to his calling.

When the time was right, the same door that locked him in became the door God used to bring him out.

Wisdom Key: When you feel forgotten, God is forming you for remembrance.

Prayer:

Lord,

Thank You for the times when obedience costs more than comfort. Thank You for shaping me in places I do not understand.

Help me trust Your hand even when I cannot trace it. Refine my heart in the quiet places.

Teach me to embrace the dungeon as Your workshop and the rejection as Your redirection.

May I serve with humility and love even when forgotten. Let Your presence sustain me as it did Joseph, and prepare me for the promise You have spoken.

In Jesus' name, Amen.

Wisdom Keys

- Obedience may close doors before it opens destiny.

- God's steadfast love remains when every earthly support is gone.

- The same rejection that wounds you may be the road that raises you.

- Presence is the true measure of prosperity.

- What imprisons you today may introduce you to tomorrow's purpose.

- Rejection is often God's redirection.

Chapter 6 — When the Gift Speaks

"A man's gift maketh room for him, and bringeth him before great men." — **Proverbs 18:16**

"And Joseph answered Pharaoh, saying, It is not in me: God shall give Pharaoh an answer of peace." — **Genesis 41:16**

Spiritual Principle

When man forgets you, God remembers your gift—and when God remembers your gift, He reveals your purpose.

Opening Narrative

It had been **two full years** since Joseph interpreted the dreams of Pharaoh's chief butler and baker, and still, there was no sign of freedom.

Silence. Delay. Another day of chains. Another night in prison. And yet, Joseph remained faithful. He served with excellence in *obscurity,* trusted God without *applause,* and held on to his *integrity* in a place of invisibility.

What Joseph could not see—but what God had ordained—was that his gift was about to speak louder than his circumstances.

Pharaoh had a dream. A troubling one. None of Egypt's magicians or wise men could interpret it.

And then, like a door creaking open after years of waiting, the butler remembered. *"There is a Hebrew young man..."* he said. Joseph was summoned. Shaved. Dressed. And in one divine moment, everything changed.

But Joseph didn't rush to defend himself. He didn't beg for a second chance. When Pharaoh asked if he could interpret dreams, Joseph answered, *"It is not in me: God shall give Pharaoh an answer of peace."* **(Genesis 41:16)**

That is the voice of a man who has been *broken, tested,* and *refined.* Joseph no longer needed to prove himself—he was content to let God speak through the gift.

Leadership that lasts must come from *humility.* Joseph's time in the dungeon crushed the *arrogance of youth.* It stripped him of *entitlement* and taught him *patience, silence,* and the *power of divine timing.*

Like **Watchman Nee** often emphasized—true ministry begins only when the outer man is broken, and the life of Christ within is free to minister.

The voice of **Mike Murdock** echoes in principle here as well: your gift can open doors, but only your character can keep you in the room.

Joseph's gift made room for him—yes—but it was *his maturity, his wisdom,* and *his godly restraint* that elevated him to govern Egypt.

Every divine assignment is connected to a problem God wants to solve through you.

Your gift is not random—it's a key designed to unlock relief, direction, or breakthrough for someone in crisis. Joseph's assignment was not to the palace itself, but to Pharaoh's problem. His wisdom was the answer to a famine that threatened nations.

Likewise, your purpose will always find expression in meeting needs. God will send you where *confusion reigns, where wisdom is lacking, or where hearts are broken.* You are the vessel He chooses to demonstrate His solution.

When you understand that your gift is the answer to someone's problem, your perspective changes.

You stop competing and start completing. You stop chasing positions and start discerning purpose. The need you are most burdened by is often the very clue to where your divine assignment lies.

Wisdom Key: God hides your promotion inside a problem. The moment you discern the problem you were created to solve; destiny begins to unfold.

The commentary reminds us that Joseph's interpretation of Pharaoh's dream was not just insightful—it was **prophetic strategy.**

He did not merely diagnose the problem; he presented a solution. Joseph's wisdom positioned him to manage an entire nation's resources through one of history's greatest famines.

God used Joseph's spiritual gift in a secular environment. He wasn't promoted within a synagogue but elevated in a palace.

This teaches us something vital: the Holy Spirit's wisdom can *influence kings, policies, and nations* when it is properly stewarded.

God had not forgotten Joseph. God had been preparing Pharaoh to need him. Sometimes, God does not change your circumstances—He changes the environment until it requires what He placed in you.

Observation — What Do We See?

- **God's clock, not man's calendar:** *"Two full years"* pass **(Gen. 41:1)** before the gift is summoned. *Delay is not denial.*

- **Providence through remembrance:** The butler *"remembered"* at the exact moment Pharaoh needed heaven's voice.

- **Humility at the microphone:** "It is not in me"—Joseph redirects credit before offering counsel.

- **Revelation with administration:** Joseph interprets the dream and presents a national strategy (Gen. 41:33-36).

- **Gift → Room → Role:** The gift opens the door; character keeps him in the room; wisdom defines his role.

Wisdom Key: The gift speaks clearest when self is silent.

Interpretation — What Did It Mean Then?

In Egypt, dreams were revered as *divine messages,* yet the empire's experts were powerless. Joseph stood as a Spirit-filled witness in a palace of power, showing that true interpretation *"belongs to God."*

His rise teaches that:

- **Divine wisdom is missional:** God positions His people where crises expose the limits of human counsel.

- **Promotion follows preparation:** Years of hidden obedience prepared Joseph to speak once and be trusted forever.

- **God serves nations through sanctified vessels:** Holiness in obscurity makes wisdom credible in public.

Theology of the Gift

A gift is grace on assignment—God's voice through a willing vessel, not a prop for personal validation.

- **Source:** "It is not in me."

- **Stewardship:** Gifts must be governed by humility and consecration.

- **Scope:** Gifts are for service, not spotlight—for solving problems, not seeking platforms.

- **Sustainability:** Gifts open doors; character keeps you there.

Wisdom Key: A pure gift flows from a purified heart.

Theological Principles

1. **God Times the Release of the Gift.** He aligns need with anointing.

2. **Humility Is the Gateway of Authority.** Credit given to God becomes credibility before men.

3. **Revelation Must Become Strategy.** True prophetic insight births wise solutions.

4. **Secular Spaces Are Kingdom Stages.** God often displays His wisdom in unexpected environments.

5. **Character Carries What the Gift Creates.** Integrity sustains what revelation begins.

Spiritual Insight — When Silence Breaks

Silence purified Joseph's motives. By the time the call came, he didn't crave a platform—he carried a purpose.

The need summoned the gift. That is heaven's order.

Wisdom Key: Gifts respond to assignment, not ambition.

Commentary Reflection

Joseph didn't just interpret Pharaoh's dream—he released prophetic strategy. His Spirit-led plan preserved life.

Pharaoh recognized God's hand, saying, *"Can we find such a one as this, a man in whom the Spirit of God is?"* **(Gen. 41:38).**

True prophetic ministry not only announces but administers. *It builds. It blesses. It bears fruit.*

Application — What Does It Mean for Us Today?

- **Serve in obscurity:** Excellence in hidden places trains your gift to serve, not perform.

- **Defer the glory:** Start with *"It is not in me."* God's presence is the true credential.

- **Solve real problems:** Use your gift to bring peace and order where there is confusion.

- **Stay usable, not just visible:** Let God shape environments until they require what He's placed in you.

- **Lead with restraint:** The door your gift opens will demand the discipline your trials forged.

Modern Parallels: *The teacher* whose unseen lessons shape a generation; *the intercessor* who moves mountains in prayer; *the administrator* whose Spirit-led systems preserve communities in crisis.

Reflective Questions:

1. Are you willing to serve faithfully in hidden places while waiting for your gift to speak?

2. What specific problem, need, or burden has God repeatedly placed on your heart—and could this be the very area your gift was created to solve?

   Take a moment to pray and write down the needs that move you most deeply. Within that burden may lie the blueprint of your divine assignment.

3. How has your time in isolation shaped your ability to minister or lead?

4. Do you recognize when God is using your gift for His glory, not your promotion?

5. What does it mean to let your gift speak without striving to be seen?

6. How can you steward your gifting with humility, as Joseph did?

Reflective Summary:

Joseph's elevation was not sudden—it was the manifestation of years of silent obedience, testing, and inner growth. His gift did not just make room for him; it positioned him to be a vessel of divine wisdom in a crisis.

The same gift he used in prison became the key that unlocked the doors of Pharaoh's palace. But it was not the gift alone—it was the maturity formed in secret, the humility refined in pain, and the obedience tested in rejection that made him fit for the role.

God does not forget those who serve in the shadows. He exalts in due season. When the time is right, your gift will speak—and it will not whisper. It will declare the glory of God.

Wisdom Keys

- Delay matures the voice your gift will one day carry.

- Gifts open doors; character earns trust; wisdom sustains influence.

- "It is not in me" is the sound of a safe vessel.

- Revelation that doesn't become strategy is unfinished stewardship.

- When God changes the environment to need your gift, no rival can replace you.

- The gift that once brought rejection will one day redeem a nation.

Prayer:

Father, I thank You that the gift You've placed in me is not wasted—even when hidden.

Teach me to wait with faith, to serve with joy, and to trust You with timing.

Help me to steward what You've placed in me with integrity and humility.

May my gift speak only when You say it's time—and may it speak for Your glory alone.

In Jesus' name, Amen.

Chapter 7: Refined to Rise — When You Become the Vessel

"He sent a man before them, even Joseph, who was sold for a servant:

Whose feet they hurt with fetters: he was laid in iron."

— Psalm 105:17–18

Before Joseph ever stood in Pharaoh's court, he was sent by God—not promoted, but processed.

He didn't arrive in Egypt with fanfare. He was sold. Shackled. Bound in chains. His feet hurt with iron, and his soul wrestled with silence. And yet, Scripture doesn't say he was abandoned—it says he was **sent.**

This changes everything. Joseph wasn't just surviving hardship—he was being forged by it. And in that furnace of *rejection, betrayal,* and *confinement,* something greater was happening. He was being refined to rise.

This is the chapter of **transformation**—not just from servant to ruler, but from wounded son to trustworthy vessel. This is where refinement becomes readiness. And this is where God's true servants are revealed.

Before Joseph could feed a nation, he had to forgive a family. And not just forgive them—but *welcome them, feed them, and reassure them.* That's the sign of a vessel truly refined.

Refinement isn't complete until you can bless what once broke you.

Observation — What Do You See?

Psalm 105:17–18 gives a divine summary of Joseph's journey:

"He sent a man before them, even Joseph, who was sold for a servant:

Whose feet they hurt with fetters: he was laid in iron."

Key Words / Frequency / Emphasis

- **Sent** — God's initiative: Joseph was not abandoned but assigned.

- **Sold** — human action used for divine direction.

- **Fetters / Iron** — pressure that forged endurance.

- **Contrast:** sent / sold hurt / helped bound / blessed — the rhythm of providence through paradox.

Observation Summary:

Before Joseph became the ruler, he was the servant. Before he fed nations, he served households.

The pattern of his life reveals that refinement begins in service and ends in stewardship.

Interpretation — What Did It Mean Then?

Psalm 105 reframes Joseph's pain as purpose. He was not merely enduring captivity—he was being trained for compassion.

At seventeen he served his father as a messenger. In Potiphar's house, he served with excellence until falsely accused. In prison, he served the butler and the baker by interpreting their dreams. In Pharaoh's court, he served an entire nation through divine wisdom.

Each setting demanded greater humility, deeper wisdom, and cleaner motives.

Joseph's greatness was not discovered in the palace; it was developed in the places where he served unseen.

Observation Key: Every act of servanthood was a classroom for leadership. God was not preparing a celebrity—He was forming a servant-king.

Theological Principles

1. **Providence and Process** — God's purpose is accomplished through pressure.

2. **Refinement Before Responsibility** — Character must be forged before crowns can be worn.

3. **Promotion Is Expanded Service** — Elevation multiplies assignment, not applause.

4. **Servanthood Is the Secret of Sustained Success** — The heart that swept Potiphar's floor governed Pharaoh's throne.

5. **Forgiveness Is the Final Proof of Refinement** — When you can bless what broke you, you're ready to lead.

Jesus said, *"He that would be great among you, let him be your servant."* — **Matthew 20:26**

This timeless truth echoes through Joseph's life. Every level of his promotion was a deeper call to serve.

True greatness is never measured by the throne you occupy, but by the people you lift.

Wisdom Key: If your dream only benefits you, it's ambition. If it blesses others, **it's assignment.**

Application — What Does It Mean for Us Today?

- See every environment as a training ground. Serve where you stand.

- Ask, Who is God calling me to help right now? That is where your anointing will flow.

- When you can serve without recognition, God can trust you with influence.

- Don't pray for promotion—pray for the heart that can handle it.

- Let refinement teach you to lead through empathy, not ego.

Prayer Focus: Lord, teach me to serve faithfully in every stage of my life. Make my promotion an expansion of my purpose, not an escape from pressure.

Principles Echoing Mike Murdock

- Every assignment exists to solve a problem. Joseph's wisdom was the answer to famine.

- God hides promotion inside a problem. Pharaoh's crisis uncovered Joseph's calling.

- The problem you solve determines the favor you receive.

- Your reaction to a problem reveals your readiness. Joseph responded with excellence, not ego.

- Refinement teaches discernment. Before you can recognize opportunity, you must recognize need.

Wisdom Key: Your gift identifies you, but your response to problems defines you.

Wisdom Key: Every servant refined by fire becomes a vessel fit to carry solutions.

Summary Thought

Joseph's life demonstrates that the pathway to greatness is paved with service.

He rose not because he sought thrones but because he stayed faithful in tasks.

Each chain, chore, and challenge shaped the vessel that would one day save a nation.

When refinement becomes readiness, servanthood becomes sovereignty.

The Shift from Fire to Fruit

Fire, in God's hands, is never wasted. It melts pride. It breaks self-will. It destroys ego. But it also purifies, shapes, and reveals.

Joseph's journey teaches us that you know you're ready not when you're out of the fire, but when the fire no longer controls your response.

He could have come out of the dungeon bitter. He could have used his platform for revenge. He could have told Pharaoh everything he'd suffered.

But instead, he interpreted a dream, gave glory to God, and offered a plan to save a nation.

He didn't announce his healing—he walked in it.

This is the hallmark of maturity:

Before Joseph could feed a nation, he had to forgive a family. And not just forgive them—but welcome them, feed them, and reassure them.

That's the sign of a vessel truly refined.

Neuroscience and Spiritual Maturity

Joseph was only seventeen when he entered Egypt—his body growing into manhood, but his mind still maturing.

According to modern neuroscience, **the frontal cortex**—the region responsible for *decision-making, wisdom, and emotional control*—doesn't fully develop until around the age of **twenty-five.**

This biological truth underscores a spiritual reality: though Joseph's dream was divine, his character needed shaping.

God did not rush the process. He waited until Joseph reached **thirty years old**—a biblical number often associated with maturity and readiness—before elevating him to rulership **(Genesis 41:46).**

Behavioral Science and Spiritual Formation

God was not just waiting for age to pass. He was waiting on spiritual readiness. *The dungeon, the rejection, the silence*—these were not delays but divine tools to mature both his brain and his spirit.

And in all that time God was molding and shaping him, Joseph was serving.

All his reflections, neurons, and brain activities knew was to serve.

Modern behavioral science helps us understand what Scripture has always taught: *repeated actions form internal patterns.*

Every act of *humility, obedience, or compassion* strengthens corresponding pathways in the brain. Neuroscientists call this **"neuroplasticity"**—the brain's ability to reorganize itself by forming new neural connections through repeated experience.

The Law of Neural Pathways

When Joseph chose to serve instead of sulk, he wasn't just being faithful—he was training his mind toward faithfulness.

Each act of *service* in Potiphar's house, each display of *patience* in prison, and each *interpretation offered with humility* was reinforcing the same mental and spiritual circuit: obedience without recognition.

Psychologists call this process *"behavioral conditioning."* It's the same principle Paul describes spiritually in **Romans 12:2:**

"Be transformed by the renewing of your mind."

Repeated behavior, aligned with godly purpose, reshapes emotional response. Over time, Joseph's instincts became **service-oriented** rather than self-centered.

His neural patterns no longer sought validation—they sought **usefulness.** His reward center (the brain's limbic system) was retrained to find joy not in applause but in obedience.

The Habit of Serving

Behavioral theorists such as **B. F. Skinner** observed that consistent behavior under consistent reinforcement creates enduring patterns.

But in Joseph's case, the "reinforcement" wasn't material—it was spiritual.

Every time he served, even in obscurity, he received divine affirmation in the form of *peace, purpose, and presence.*

That means service became both his coping mechanism and his worship. His brain learned what his spirit already knew: *"Whatever you do, do it heartily, as unto the Lord."* **(Colossians 3:23)**

Over years of repetition, Joseph's behavior was no longer reactionary—**it was reflexive.**

His brain chemistry and emotional responses were conformed to his calling.

By the time Pharaoh summoned him, Joseph didn't have to "rise to the occasion"—he simply continued what he had been doing all along: serving with excellence.

The Spiritual-Behavioral Principle

What you practice in private becomes your posture in public.

When Joseph served without recognition, God was wiring him for leadership.

When he chose *gratitude* over bitterness, *humility* over pride, and *diligence* over despair, those choices became neurological patterns of grace.

Modern behavioral psychology would call this *"cognitive restructuring"*—replacing old thought patterns *(fear, resentment, entitlement)* with new, resilient ones *(faith, gratitude, purpose)*.

But in spiritual language, we call it **transformation.**

Joseph's mind and spirit were becoming one—a sanctified integration where thought, emotion, and behavior all aligned with divine purpose.

Wisdom Key: When you make servanthood your habit, God makes leadership your inheritance.

Reflection Thought

God wasn't simply aging Joseph—He was wiring him for wisdom.

Years of faithful service in low places created mental pathways of endurance, emotional regulation, and empathy—the very traits required to sustain influence without pride.

Joseph didn't just think like a servant; he became one *in mind, heart, and habit.*

So, by the time God opened the palace doors, Joseph's brain and spirit were already synchronized for service.

He didn't have to learn how to lead—he had been living it.

Joseph wasn't just a dreamer anymore. He was becoming a man molded by fire, discipline, and wisdom.

The Evidence of Refinement

The evidence that Joseph was truly refined was found in how he responded when he had the power to retaliate—and chose instead to serve:

- He could weep.

- He could bless.

- He could lead with a clean heart.

Joseph didn't just survive hardship—he was shaped by it. He didn't just go through the process—he let the process go through him.

Refinement isn't complete until you can bless what once broke you.

You're Not Just a Survivor—You're a Vessel

Too many today survive hardship but carry bitterness into their promotion. Not Joseph. And not you—not if you let God finish what He started.

The furnace did not kill him—it revealed him. He came out with:

- Wisdom instead of wounds

- Grace instead of grudges

- Purpose instead of pain

This is what it means to become the vessel. The process doesn't just prepare you for the platform—it prepares you for the people.

Joseph could stand before Pharaoh, not because he escaped the fire, but because he was changed by it. He was no longer just carrying a dream— he was carrying the character to fulfill it.

Let Us Not Make the Same Mistake

Let us not overlook the purpose of refinement.

Let us not seek the palace before we've surrendered in the prison.

Let us not step into influence while still bleeding from our offense.

God refines us so that when the door opens, we walk through it healed, whole, and ready—not just to rule, but to restore.

Reflective Questions:

1. Can you identify a moment in your life when refinement shifted into readiness?

2. Are you carrying old wounds into your new season—or have you truly released them?

3. What relationships or memories do you need to bless instead of curse?

4. How is God asking you to serve with clean hands and a pure heart?

5. Are you ready to move from being a survivor to being a vessel?

Reflective Summary:

Chapter 7 is not about endurance alone—it's about emergence. Joseph emerged from his trials not just alive, but anointed, aware, and appointed.

He no longer needed affirmation from others—he was grounded in the God who refined him.

This is where God wants to bring all His servants—not just through the fire, but **transformed by it.**

You are not just being tested—you are being tempered.

You are not just being broken—you are being built.

And when God is finished, you won't just carry a dream—you'll become the kind of vessel through which others are sustained.

Jesus said, *"He that would be great among you, let him be your servant."* — **Matthew 20:26**

True greatness is found not in being served, but in serving. Joseph's rise was not the reward of endurance—it was the fruit of a servant's heart refined by fire.

Greatness is never self-made; it is **Spirit-formed** in those who choose *humility* over honor, *compassion* over competition, and *service* over status.

When you embrace the posture of a servant, you step into the likeness of Christ Himself—the ultimate example of divine greatness through selfless love.

Prayer:

Father,

Thank You for every fire that shaped me, every silence that taught me, and every moment of rejection that led me closer to You.

Refine my heart, so that I carry purpose instead of pain.

Let me walk through every door You open with humility, forgiveness, and faith.

Remove every residue of bitterness, pride, and fear.

Make me not just a survivor, but a vessel—fit to serve, fit to lead, and fit to glorify You.

In Jesus' name, Amen.

Chapter 8 — From the Prison to the Palace: Prepared for Purpose

"Then Pharaoh sent and called Joseph, and they brought him hastily out of the dungeon... And Pharaoh said unto Joseph, 'See, I have set thee over all the land of Egypt.'" — **Genesis 41:14, 41**

"Before Joseph wore a crown, he wore chains." — **You Were Born for More**

Step 1: Observation — What Happened Then

Joseph's transformation from prisoner to prime minister is one of the greatest turning points in Scripture. In one day, God reversed years of injustice, but the reversal didn't come without refinement.

Egypt's throne was powerful, but so was the prison. Both were classrooms. Joseph's story is not about escaping hardship—it's about being educated by it.

He entered Egypt as a slave, served faithfully in Potiphar's house, was falsely accused, imprisoned, and then elevated to the second-highest position in the nation. The same God who gave him dreams as a teenager was now manifesting those dreams through maturity.

Step 2: Interpretation — What It Meant Then

Joseph's story reveals the nature of divine assignments. Every calling includes:

1. **A dream** — the revelation of destiny.

2. **A delay** — the testing of obedience.

3. **A development** — the formation of character.

4. **A demonstration** — the public unveiling of purpose.

God was not merely rescuing Joseph; He was repositioning him for kingdom responsibility. Joseph's elevation was not about comfort—it was about covenant.

Through his stewardship, Israel's lineage would be preserved. The palace wasn't the prize; purpose was.

Step 3: Theological Principle — What It Teaches Us About God

Every biblical narrative reveals something about God's nature and man's relationship with Him. From Joseph's story, we learn:

1. **God's providence works through process.** He uses time, testing, and training to align your readiness with your revelation.

2. **God values integrity over immediacy.** He would rather delay your destiny than destroy it through immaturity.

3. **God's promotion is purposeful.**
   Elevation in God's kingdom is never about personal achievement but about redemptive assignment.

4. **God allows adversity to authenticate anointing.** Where there is real purpose, there will be real pressure.

As The Assignment teaches, the anointing does not remove adversity—it reveals readiness. Your assignment will always expose what your anointing has prepared you to overcome.

Step 4: Application — What It Means for Us Today

The principles that elevated Joseph still apply today. You can't rush spiritual maturity, skip adversity, or buy character.

1. The Dream Requires Development

Your calling will always exceed your current capacity. Like Joseph, your early enthusiasm must be tempered by endurance. Dreams begin as revelation but mature through responsibility.

2. The Anointing Attracts Adversity

Opposition is the certificate of authenticity for every anointed believer. The proof of divine favor is not the absence of storms but the grace to stand through them.

3. The Assignment Demands Alignment

God will not entrust influence to a divided heart. Before Joseph could rule Egypt, he had to learn to rule his own spirit. The Spirit-filled life is not about control—it's about character.

4. The Palace Requires Stewardship

Success reveals what suffering refined. In the prison, Joseph learned humility; in the palace, he practiced accountability. Leadership is never ownership—it's management on God's behalf.

5. The Adversity Prepares You for the Audience

Every hidden season trains you for visibility. Before you speak to Pharaohs, you must first interpret dreams in secret. God hides His greatest voices until they've been purged of pride.

Maturity by Design

By the time Joseph stood before Pharaoh, he was **thirty**—both biologically and spiritually ready.

Science tells us that this is when the human brain reaches maturity; Scripture tells us it's when *priests, kings,* and even *Christ* began public ministry.

God aligns human development with divine destiny.

He waits until your **mind can manage your mantle.**

Divine Vindication

Joseph's story reminds us that vindication is God's responsibility, not ours. He did not manipulate his way into Pharaoh's favor; he served his way there. When the butler remembered his name, it was because Heaven whispered it.

Promotion comes when private excellence meets public opportunity. The same faithfulness that interpreted dreams in prison now administered wisdom in a palace.

Principle: God does not promote potential—He promotes proof.

Faith in a Secular Palace

Joseph's assignment was not inside a sanctuary but within a system. God trusted him with *policy, agriculture,* and *economics* because **spiritual wisdom** is not limited to religious spaces.

Observation: God will often place His children in ungodly environments to demonstrate godly excellence.

Interpretation: Light shines brightest in dark places.

Theological Principle: The Spirit's wisdom is relevant in every field—*education, business, politics, and justice.*

Application: Let your work ethic become your witness. When you excel in your craft, Heaven gains a voice in culture.

Anointing Meets Adversity

Joseph's anointing did not shield him from hardship—it sustained him through it. *Every pit, every lie, every delay* became a tool in God's hand to strengthen his endurance.

You cannot carry power without pain. The oil that anoints also costs the crushing of olives.

Modern Application:

When your life feels pressed, remember that God is extracting something pure. The crushing that breaks you before men is producing the fragrance that pleases Heaven.

The Responsibility of Promotion

Joseph's promotion came with weight. He was not given a platform for pride but a position for provision.

In times of famine, leadership is not luxury—it's service.

What God gives you to manage reveals the size of your maturity.

Kingdom Principle: Promotion is not a throne to sit on—it's a towel to serve with.

In your modern world, that means every blessing is a stewardship test. Whether you lead a family, a business, or a ministry, Heaven watches how you handle what's in your hands.

Wisdom Keys for Today

- **The proof of assignment is adversity.** What fights you the most often defines your purpose.

- **The season you despise may be preparing you for the season you desire.**

- **God hides greatness in small responsibilities.** If you can serve without spotlight, you're ready for stewardship.

- **Every environment is a test of excellence.** The way you treat today's prison determines how you'll function in tomorrow's palace.

- **Where there is order, there will be increase.** God promotes disciplined minds, not distracted hearts.

Let Us Not Make the Same Mistake

Let us not seek exposure before endurance.

Let us not demand influence without instruction.

Let us not pursue destiny without discernment.

Joseph's story warns us that **the palace will reveal what the prison didn't heal.** If you rush your process, your promotion becomes punishment. But if you submit to refinement, your destiny becomes your deliverance.

Reflective Questions:

1. What dream has God given you that still requires development?

2. How has adversity refined your understanding of your assignment?

3. Where might God be calling you to demonstrate spiritual excellence in a secular environment?

4. What disciplines must you strengthen to handle the next level of responsibility?

5. How can you serve faithfully today while waiting for tomorrow's opportunity?

Reflective Summary:

Joseph's rise from the prison to the palace was not a coincidence—it was covenant fulfillment through character formation.

His journey proves that divine destiny is not about elevation but preparation for service.

God still moves through this pattern today:

Dream → Delay → Development → Demonstration.

When your anointing meets adversity, your faith matures.

When your mind aligns with your mission, God releases increase.

When your assignment becomes your obsession, Heaven entrusts you with influence.

For the believer, every dungeon is a design studio for destiny.

Closing Insight: The anointing that attracts adversity is the same anointing that will advance you. God never promotes without purpose, and He never prepares without a plan.

Prayer:

Father,

Thank You for the dream that awakens destiny within us.

Teach us to endure the development, embrace the adversity, and discern our assignment.

Align our thoughts with Your truth, our emotions with Your Spirit, and our actions with Your will.

When You elevate us, keep us humble. When You use us, keep us pure.

May our lives reflect Joseph's wisdom, Jesus' character, and the Holy Ghost's power.

In Jesus' name, Amen.

Chapter 9 — The Weight of Responsibility: Walking in What You Were Called For

"And Joseph was thirty years old when he stood before Pharaoh king of Egypt. And Joseph went out from the presence of Pharaoh, and went throughout all the land of Egypt." — **Genesis 41:46**

"Responsibility is not the end of the calling — it is the evidence that the calling was real." — **You Were Born for More**

Observation — What Happened Then

Joseph was no longer the forgotten prisoner. The same hands that once turned the keys of confinement now carried the seal of authority.

He stood before Pharaoh, clothed in linen, entrusted with Egypt's destiny—and immediately went out throughout all the land.

He did not linger for applause; he stepped into assignment. The palace did not make Joseph—it revealed the man the prison had forged. God's promotion is never a decoration; it is delegation.

Commentary Note

According to the **Tyndale Old Testament Commentary** and the **New Interpreter's Bible,** Joseph's promotion in **Genesis 41:46** signifies far more than personal advancement. In the ancient Near Eastern world, a king's second-in-command served as both vizier and guardian of resources—a position of national trust and sacred duty.

Joseph's immediate departure *"throughout all the land of Egypt"* illustrates his understanding that leadership in God's order is not ceremonial but **functional.** His actions display *no vanity, no delay, no self-glorification*—**only readiness.**

This verse reveals a divine rhythm repeated throughout Scripture: **calling → cleansing → commissioning.**

Moses tended sheep before leading people. **David** ruled sheep before ruling Israel. **Jesus** endured wilderness temptation before ministering to multitudes.

Every true leader is refined in private before being revealed in power.

Interpretation — What It Meant Then

Joseph's elevation was heaven's endorsement of hidden faithfulness. **The New Interpreter's Bible** describes it as a divine act of trust—God handing purpose to a purified vessel.

Power without character corrupts, but power governed by **humility** becomes ministry.

Joseph's assignment was **national survival,** not personal success. What began as a dream of influence had matured into a burden of responsibility.

Kingdom Principle: Elevation is not the end of preparation; it is the beginning of accountability.

Theological Principles — What It Reveals About God

1. **God's timing reveals His trust.** Delay is never denial—it is design for maturity.

2. **God entrusts influence to the faithful.** The palace is reserved for those who stayed pure in the prison.

3. **God's wisdom transcends walls.** The Spirit who interprets dreams also engineers strategy.

4. **God measures leaders by stewardship, not status.** His definition of greatness is servanthood.

Leading in Crisis

Joseph faced a global famine—an agricultural, political, and humanitarian crisis. Yet his leadership was *calm, calculated,* and *Spirit-led.* He transformed *revelation* into regulation, *prophecy* into policy.

Leadership in crisis demands foresight birthed from fellowship. Joseph's plan—storing grain during years of plenty—was divine wisdom dressed in practical work.

Wisdom Key: Foresight is the fruit of intimacy with God.

When leaders pray before acting, strategy becomes stewardship.

The Anatomy of Authority

Joseph's authority was recognized, not requested. Pharaoh said, *"Can we find such a man, in whom is the Spirit of God?"* Authority that flows from the Spirit does not need validation—it bears its own witness.

Years of confinement had killed entitlement. Joseph ruled with **empathy,** not ego; with **restraint,** not reaction. He listened before he led.

Spiritual Law: You can only lead to the degree that you have learned to listen.

Stewardship in Elevation

The first act of Joseph's promotion was administration. He went to work. Every storehouse built was a sermon on diligence. Every measured grain testified that divine revelation must manifest in daily responsibility.

Theological Truth: The anointing is not given for applause but for administration.

Worship is expressed not only in words but in work done well.

Murdock-Style Principle: God promotes servants, not celebrities; stewardship sustains what favor starts.

Servanthood in Leadership

The responsibility we carry as leaders must be taken seriously. When God entrusts you with influence, He entrusts you with souls. Eternity hangs in the balance of every decision we make.

For those in church leadership, this is not a career—it is a covenant. The pulpit is not a platform for performance; it is a place of accountability. Souls can stumble when shepherds grow careless.

In an age where ministry is often mistaken for celebrity, we must return to Christ's example:

"The Son of Man did not come to be served, but to serve." **(Matthew 20:28)**

Joseph embodied that principle. Though arrayed like a ruler, he thought like a servant. His crown was made of humility, not hierarchy.

Spiritual Principle: The higher God lifts you, the lower you must bow.

True leadership is sacrificial, not self-exalting. We are *ambassadors,* not aristocrats. The moment a minister begins to act like *royalty* instead of a *shepherd,* the flock becomes endangered.

Elevation without humility becomes exploitation.

Leadership without love becomes lordship.

Ministry without mercy becomes manipulation.

God is calling this generation back to the towel, not the throne. Like Joseph, we must go out *"throughout all the land"*—to feed, not to flaunt.

Wisdom Key: The true crown of leadership is a clean conscience before God.

The Power of Naming — Healing in the Midst of Responsibility

Joseph named his sons **Manasseh** ("God made me forget") and **Ephraim** ("God made me fruitful").

Manasseh signified release; **Ephraim** represented redemption.

He named them after his promotion to remind himself that prosperity is pointless without purity of heart. Forgetting meant freedom from resentment, not erasure of memory.

Principle: Fruitfulness follows forgiveness.

You cannot lead effectively while living emotionally in the past.

The Leader Who Could Forgive

The ultimate test of spiritual authority came when Joseph's brothers bowed before him. He had the power to imprison them as they once imprisoned him. Instead, he chose mercy.

Forgiveness is not weakness—it is governance of the soul.

He proved that real power is the ability to bless what once broke you.

Wisdom Key: Unforgiveness disqualifies you from the future you pray for.

The Neuroscience of Responsibility

Modern research shows that sustained responsibility rewires the brain toward *empathy* and *foresight*. Spiritually, sustained obedience does the same—it rewires the soul for discernment.

Joseph's years of consistency built neural and spiritual endurance. Each act of obedience became muscle memory for maturity. He didn't merely react—he responded from refinement.

Spiritual Truth: Maturity is measured by how you manage pressure, not how you pursue pleasure.

The Weight of Responsibility

Joseph carried the weight of nations, yet Scripture records no complaint. He saw responsibility not as a burden but as a blessing—proof that God trusted him.

Murdock Principle: What you manage determines what God multiplies.

Responsibility is worship in motion—the daily act of managing what belongs to God with excellence and reverence.

Every leader will one day give account, not for how high he rose, but for how faithfully he served.

Biblical Stewardship Defined

Biblical stewardship is the divinely entrusted responsibility to manage God's resources—*His people, gifts, time, truth, and creation*—according to His will and for His glory.

It is the understanding that everything belongs to God and that we, as His servants, are caretakers rather than owners.

Expanded Explanation

Stewardship in Scripture flows from the truth of
Psalm 24:1 —

*"The earth is the Lord's, and the fullness
thereof; the world, and they that dwell therein."*

Because all things belong to God, every
blessing—whether *material, spiritual,* or
relational—is a trust, not a possession.

A steward is accountable to the Owner for how
he handles what has been placed in his hands.

In the New Testament, Jesus uses the parable of the talents **(Matthew 25:14–30)** to illustrate this principle. Each servant was given something *"according to his ability,"* not to own, but to multiply for the master's benefit. The reward or rebuke came based on faithfulness, not fame.

Thus, biblical stewardship is not limited to money or ministry—it includes ***time, influence, opportunities, spiritual gifts, revelation, relationships, and authority.***

It asks one question above all others:

"Am I managing what God gave me in a way that reflects His character and advances His purpose?"

Core Principles of Biblical Stewardship

1. God is the Owner.

We possess nothing; we are entrusted with everything **(1 Chronicles 29:11–12).**

2. We are Managers, not Masters.

Our role is to care for and cultivate what belongs to God **(Genesis 2:15).**

3. Faithfulness is the Standard.

God evaluates stewardship by obedience, not outcome **(1 Corinthians 4:2).**

4. **Stewardship Extends Beyond Resources.**

   It includes influence, authority, and relationships **(Luke 16:10–12).**

5. **Accountability is Certain.**

   Every steward must one day give an account of his management **(Romans 14:12).**

6. **The Goal is God's Glory.**

   True stewardship directs attention away from the steward and toward the Owner **(1 Peter 4:10–11).**

Application

When you understand stewardship, leadership changes.

The question is no longer "What do I want to build?" but "What has God placed in my hands to *protect, develop, and return to Him with increase?*"

Joseph modeled this perfectly. He governed Egypt not as Pharaoh's servant but as God's steward. His leadership fed nations, reconciled families, and preserved the covenant line through which Christ would come.

Summary Statement

Biblical stewardship is the sacred trust of managing what belongs to God in a way *that honors His ownership, reflects His character, serves His people, and fulfills His purpose.*

Let Us Not Make the Same Mistake

Let us not seek crowns without crosses or titles without tears. The palace will magnify whatever the prison refined.

If pride remains, power will expose it; if humility rules, influence will expand it.

Joseph thrived because Egypt never ruled him. He ruled Egypt by ruling himself.

Wisdom Key: The true measure of maturity is not how much power you gain but how much purity you keep while holding it.

Reflective Questions:

1. How does Joseph's response to promotion reveal spiritual maturity?

2. What does servant-leadership look like in your present calling?

3. How are you stewarding the souls or responsibilities God has placed under your care?

4. What pain or pride must you release to lead with purity?

5. How can you model Joseph's humility and foresight in your ministry or vocation?

Reflective Summary:

Joseph's story teaches that responsibility is the currency of divine trust. His **faithfulness** in obscurity became his **credibility** in influence. He governed a nation because he first governed his heart.

For leaders today, the lesson is clear: we are **servants** before we are stewards, **shepherds** before we are supervisors.

The call to leadership is not a call to prominence but to proximity with God—to carry His heart for His people.

When God elevates you, He is not exalting your name; He is extending His hand through yours.

The palace is not a privilege—it is a proving ground for character.

Closing Insight: When your heart stays humble, Heaven keeps trusting you. The greatest weight a leader carries is not power—it is responsibility for souls.

Leadership Creed: Commitments of a Godly Steward

1. I will remember that every opportunity is a trust, not a trophy.

2. I will lead from the towel, not the throne.

3. I will guard my heart more than I guard my title.

4. I will serve with integrity, even when unseen.

5. I will forgive quickly, love deeply, and speak truthfully.

6. I will measure success by faithfulness, not fame.

7. I will lead in such a way that when God looks for a steward, He can trust me again.

Prayer:

Father,

Thank You for trusting us with the care of others.

Teach us to lead from the posture of a servant and the heart of a shepherd.

Help us remember that every title is temporary, but every soul is eternal. Deliver us from pride, distraction, and self-promotion.

Let our leadership reflect Your compassion, Your truth, and Your integrity.

May we carry the towel before we ever touch the throne, and may every decision we make bring life to those You've assigned to our care.

In Jesus' name, Amen.

Chapter 10: The Legacy of Obedience — When Favor Doesn't Make You Forget

"And Joseph said unto his brethren, I die: and God will surely visit you, and bring you out of this land unto the land which he sware to Abraham, to Isaac, and to Jacob."

— Genesis 50:24

Spiritual Principle

True favor does not make you forget where God found you—it reminds you to redeem where He sent you.

The Test of Legacy

Joseph had learned to govern a nation—but now he had to govern his own heart.

The brothers who betrayed him stood before him, trembling. The past was no longer behind him— it was staring him in the face.

Would he retaliate, or would he reveal the legacy of obedience?

Some men rise to power and forget where they came from. Joseph didn't. He never let the palace erase the process. He never let the robe of royalty cover the wounds that made him wise.

Even with wealth, prestige, and a new Egyptian name, Joseph remained a Hebrew at heart—a man formed in the furnace of affliction, shaped in the silence of obscurity, and called to a legacy that stretched beyond his lifetime.

He Remembered the Promise

As Joseph neared death, he didn't boast of what he built; he spoke of what God promised.

"God will surely visit you," he said—a declaration that Egypt, though prosperous, was not home. His faith looked forward. His request that his bones be carried to Canaan was a living prophecy: "Don't bury me in my blessing—carry me into the promise."

This was the voice of a man who refused to confuse provision with promise. He understood that every earthly success must bow to eternal purpose.

The Emotional Test of Obedience

Joseph's greatest test was not interpreting Pharaoh's dream or managing the famine.

It was confronting the faces that once mocked his own.

When his brothers bowed before him, Joseph's body stood in power, but his heart trembled in memory. Decades of pain and progress collided in a single moment. He wept privately—his tears the language of a soul processing trauma without bitterness.

Psychological Insight

Modern psychology calls this integration: *the mind's ability to reconcile pain with purpose.*

Unresolved trauma repeats itself; healed trauma redeems itself.

Joseph's tears were not weakness—they were release. **Forgiveness** does not erase memory; it **transforms it**. Emotional maturity is the ability to remember accurately without reliving destructively.

What Joseph displayed was **post-traumatic growth**—the psychological transformation that follows suffering when the soul chooses meaning over misery. His restraint revealed emotional intelligence refined through divine intimacy.

Power Did Not Corrupt Him

Joseph held the keys to the kingdom. With one decree, he could have reversed the injustice of his youth. Yet power didn't corrupt him—it clarified him.

The most powerful man in Egypt possessed the most purified heart.

He forgave those who hurt him. He provided for those who betrayed him.

He blessed those who once cursed him.

Psychologically, power often tempts the wounded to seek retribution. But Joseph proved that healing had replaced hatred. His leadership was not reactionary; **it was redemptive.**

He Blessed a Generation

Joseph's influence extended beyond policy; it became **pastoral.**

He sustained Egypt and preserved Israel—the covenant line of the Messiah.

His stewardship of grain became a stewardship of grace.

The **New Interpreter's Bible** observes that Joseph's story reveals how *"God works redemptively through human suffering."*

His legacy was not his title—it was his testimony.

He served faithfully in a secular system without compromise, showing that holiness can govern even in heathen halls.

He Knew the Battle Was Preparation

Joseph never idolized his pain, but he never denied it either.

He remembered the lessons carved by loss—*the pit, the false accusation, the prison's silence.*

He didn't rise in spite of hardship; he rose through it.

When his brothers finally stood before him, starving and ashamed, Joseph uttered one of Scripture's most profound statements:

"You meant it for evil, but God meant it for good." **(Genesis 50:20)**

This single verse integrates **theology** and **psychology:** pain reinterpreted through purpose.

Joseph reframed trauma into testimony. He shifted from Why did this happen to me? to What did God produce through me?

Reframing is one of the mind's highest functions—a divine echo of **Romans 8:28.**

God didn't just redeem Joseph's story; He re-authored it from the inside out.

A Wisdom Legacy

"Blessed are the merciful, for they shall obtain mercy." — **Matthew 5:7**

Joseph lived that beatitude long before Jesus spoke it.

He extended mercy not because his brothers deserved it, but because his heart had been healed.

A wisdom key in the spirit of Mike Murdock says:

"Never punish someone when God is trying to redeem them through you."

Favor gave Joseph power; obedience made him safe with it. He learned that favor is not the license to flex—it is the platform to forgive.

Watchman Nee once said that only the broken vessel can pour freely.

Joseph had been shattered, but in surrender he was sealed.

His brokenness became the channel of blessing. His tears baptized his throne.

He proved that *reconciliation* is greater than revenge, and *mercy* is mightier than memory.

His life whispers to every believer: You can walk in favor without forgetting faith.

When the Dream Finally Bowed (A Narrative Interlude)

They didn't just enter a storehouse—they crossed a threshold.

Ten men carrying a secret across the borders of famine. Ten shadows cast from one ancient sin.

And then the air shifted.

A figure rose like steel drawn from a furnace. The dream stood up in the room—and they bowed.

Joseph did not thunder. He breathed. That breath carried years of bruised nights—*pit, house, prison.*

Every scar became a sermon.

He could have condemned, but instead he commanded compassion.

He tested not to torment, but to measure repentance.

And when Judah spoke, when truth returned, the dam broke.

Joseph wept—not as a boy betrayed, but as a man reborn.

Relief did not make him small; it made him safe.

Safe to bless without boasting. Safe to feed those who failed him. Safe to speak the sentence that healed history:

"God sent me ahead of you."

Not "I made it," but "God aimed me."

Every detour was divine direction. Every delay was divine design.

The pit did not cancel the dream—it carved the vessel.

Potiphar's house did not silence his gift—it staged it.

The prison did not bury him—it positioned him.

Now, the dream bows—not to Joseph, but to God's sovereignty.

Power becomes provision. Scars become strategy.

Fulfillment isn't payback—it's purpose.

When the dream bows, the servant kneels to serve.

Observation — What Do We See?

- **Full-circle fulfillment:** The youthful dreams (bowing sheaves/stars) culminate in the brothers bowing—not for Joseph's vanity, but for their preservation **(Gen 45; 50).**

- **Reframe of harm:** Joseph explicitly contrasts human intent **("evil")** with divine intent **("good")** and frames events within God's saving purpose **("to save much people alive").**

- **Emotion with mastery:** Joseph repeatedly weeps yet never weaponizes power. Tears accompany truth; emotion serves discernment.

- **Covenant horizon:** Near death, Joseph speaks beyond Egypt's prosperity to God's visitation and the oath to *Abraham, Isaac, and Jacob*, and asks for his bones to go to Canaan **(legacy faith).**

- **Tests of transformation:** Joseph's staged tests (esp. regarding Benjamin and Judah) verify *repentance* and *repair family systems,* not to exact pain.

Keywords / Repetition / Emphasis

- **"God will surely visit you."** Repeated stress on visitation (divine intervention, covenant timing).

- **"Good / evil."** Juxtaposition highlights providence overruling malice.

- **"Remember / bones / oath."** Memory & embodiment of promise (faith that outlives the dreamer).

- **"Forgive / fear not."** Joseph repeatedly relieves fear, coupling assurance with provision.

- **Bowing / serving / feeding.** Power expressed as service, not payback.

Emphasis: Joseph's vocabulary shifts the family from **guilt** to **grace,** from **fear** to **future,** from **Egypt** to **Exodus.**

Interpretation — What Did It Mean Then?

- **For Israel:** Joseph's mercy preserved the very line through which the covenant would advance. His request about his bones functioned as a living prophecy: Egypt is way-station, not home.

- **For the brothers:** Reconciliation required truth + transformation. Judah's changed posture signals real repair, not mere remorse.

- **For the nations:** God's wisdom in one sanctified leader can steward public goods (grain, policy) while advancing redemptive history.

- **For the reader:** Suffering in Joseph is not divine neglect but divine navigation—God "aims" His servant through human wrongs to achieve a larger saving work.

Theological Principles

- **Providence Over Plotting:** Human intent is real and responsible, yet God's sovereign goodness repurposes evil toward salvation.

- **Mercy as Maturity:** The apex of spiritual growth is the capacity to forgive from strength—to steward power as bread, not as a blade.

- **Legacy Faith:** Obedience looks past present provision to promised inheritance; bones in Canaan preach faith after death.

- **Reconciliation Requires Truth:**
  Forgiveness isn't amnesia; it is grace that
  faces the past, tests transformation, and
  chooses restoration.

- **Calling Is Communal:** God-given dreams
  are rarely private trophies; they are public
  trusts for the preservation of many.

- **Christological Echo:** Joseph previews
  Christ—betrayed yet sent, exalted to save,
  feeding enemies with the bread of life,
  answering evil with good.

Application — How Should We Respond?

- **Practice redemptive reframing:** Name past harms truthfully, then ask, "How might God work good through this?" (A disciplined habit; journal it.)

- **Lead like Joseph:** Use authority (title, platform, resources) to feed, free, and heal—especially those who once feared you.

- **Build a legacy liturgy:** Identify your "bones" request—what conviction should outlive you? Write a brief "promise statement" for your family/ministry.

- **Test wisely, forgive freely:** When reconciliation is possible, pursue clear evidence of change (like Judah's) while keeping your heart ready to release.

- **Guard covenant horizons:** Celebrate today's Egypt, but plan for Canaan; align budgets, mentoring, and mission to promises bigger than comfort.

- **Integrate the heart:** When old wounds surface, allow tears without tyranny—feel fully, decide righteously. Pray, pause, then act.

Psychological Addendum (for your Pastoral Toolbox)

- **Forgiveness ≠ forgetting:** It is remembering without poison; clinically, it reduces reactivity and increases **emotional regulation.**

- **Post-traumatic growth:** Meaning-making after hardship fosters humility, empathy, and purpose—the very traits Joseph models.

- **Family systems repair:** Joseph's calibrated tests create **corrective experiences** that reset dysfunctional dynamics without repeating violence.

- **Embodied hope:** Rituals (e.g., "carry my bones") anchor future-focus; consider creating symbolic acts that point your community toward promise.

Psychological Reflection: The Anatomy of Forgiveness

Forgiveness, according to cognitive-behavioral and neurotheological research, rewires the brain's emotional circuitry.

Unforgiveness keeps **the amygdala** (the fear and anger center) inflamed, while forgiveness activates **the prefrontal cortex**—the seat of *empathy, foresight, and self-control.*

In simple terms: forgiveness heals the mind as much as the soul.

Joseph's emotional intelligence—his ability to *regulate anger, empathize with offenders*, and *reinterpret suffering*—demonstrates what psychologists call **emotional resilience**: the capacity to recover without retaliation.

This is not psychology apart from God—it is psychology sanctified by grace.

Wisdom Keys

- Forgiveness is not forgetting—it's remembering without poison.

- Favor will test whether you can be trusted with what once tempted you.

- Legacy is built when your obedience outlives your ambition.

- What others meant to bury you, God used to bless through you.

- The healed heart sees betrayal as divine redirection.

- Fulfillment in the kingdom is not applause—it's assignment.

Reflective Questions:

1. How does Joseph's final act of faith inspire you to think beyond temporary success?

2. Are you carrying your faith into the next season—or burying it in comfort?

3. What does it mean to live in favor without forgetting your foundation?

4. How can your legacy reflect obedience more than achievement?

5. In what ways has your battle prepared you for your calling?

6. If those who wounded you needed you tomorrow, how would you respond?

7. What will you name this season— **Manasseh** (forgetting pain) or **Ephraim** (fruitful in affliction)? Why?

Reflective Summary — The Reward of Remembering Right

Joseph's journey wasn't just from the pit to the palace—it was from resentment to restoration.

He didn't allow success to erase his scars or comfort to silence his calling.

He carried obedience through every elevation and died with a promise still on his tongue.

The true dreamer never stops dreaming for others.

The true leader never forgets where God found him.

The true servant never trades calling for comfort.

Let us not mistake Egypt's provision for Canaan's promise.

Let us not allow success to suffocate surrender.

The dream lives on—not because Joseph was perfect, but because he remembered.

Prayer:

Father,

Thank You for the life of Joseph—a mirror of obedience, forgiveness, and unshakable faith.

Teach me to walk in favor without pride, to lead with purity, and to remember the promise even in prosperity.

Make me safe to bless those who once broke me.

Heal the hidden places of my heart until mercy becomes my reflex.

Carry my bones toward the promise, even when Egypt feels comfortable.

May my legacy not be what I acquired, but what I obeyed.

In Jesus' name, Amen.

Chapter 11: The Dream Lives On — What God Starts, He Finishes

"Being confident of this very thing, that he which hath begun a good work in you will perform it until the day of Jesus Christ."

— Philippians 1:6

Introduction

Joseph's death was not the end of the dream—it was the transfer of faith to the next generation.

Though his body rested in Egypt, his heart was anchored in Canaan.

He lived in a palace but died with a promise.

The dream didn't die with him. It lived on through the people he preserved, the children he fathered, and the testimony he left behind.

It lived on in the bones he asked them to carry out of Egypt—the same bones **Moses** would later bear through the wilderness, a prophetic reminder that Egypt was never the final destination.

The Power of a Finished Work

Joseph's story reminds us that **what God starts, He finishes.**

The pit, the prison, and the palace were all part of the process—and so was the promise.

God never wastes a season. Every delay held design; every detour carried direction. And when He begins a work in you, even when it seems paused, heaven is still in progress.

Israel would multiply in Egypt. They would face affliction and oppression. A Pharaoh would rise who knew not Joseph—but the echo of Joseph's obedience would remain.

He had laid a foundation of faith that spoke louder than bondage. When the people wept, the story of Joseph whispered: "God has visited before—He will visit again."

A Foreshadowing of Redemption

Joseph's life was more than endurance; it was a **shadow of redemption.** Like Jesus, he was betrayed by his own, falsely accused, humiliated, and yet exalted.

He forgave those who wronged him, saved those who cursed him, and used his power to redeem rather than retaliate.

The **Life Application Study Bible** notes that Joseph's story displays the redemptive purpose of suffering—that God brings glory through grief and purpose through pain.

His journey mirrors the gospel: suffering that leads to glory, wounds that lead to healing, betrayal that leads to salvation.

Joseph prefigures Christ in at least five ways:

1. Rejected by brothers yet sent to save them.

2. Humbled before being exalted.

3. Imprisoned unjustly yet became a source of freedom.

4. Given a Gentile bride—symbolic of Christ and His Church.

5. Forgave His offenders and turned wrath into restoration.

Every scar points to the Cross, and every victory points to the Resurrection.

Faith Beyond the Grave

When Joseph said, *"God will surely visit you,"* he wasn't speaking from emotion but revelation. He believed in a future unseen yet spiritually visible. He died with hope, with vision, and above all, in faith.

Hebrews 11 records that he *"died in faith, not having received the promises, but having seen them afar off."* Faith sees beyond the finish line. His bones became **a symbol of unfinished faith**—proof that the work of God outlives the worker of God.

Legacy in Chains

Even as Israel fell into slavery, **the memory of Joseph's favor** endured. His story anchored their identity—evidence that God can raise a deliverer from disaster.

The dream was not buried; it was **planted.** Every promise that dies in faith becomes a seed for the next generation.

A Word to the Reader

Maybe your life feels stalled. Maybe your purpose feels forgotten. Maybe your dream feels delayed. But remember: if God gave the dream, He will finish what He started.

The pit cannot cancel the promise.

The prison cannot stop the purpose.

Even death cannot halt destiny.

God's work is both personal and perpetual. His timing never expires. What looks finished to man is still forming in God's plan.

The same God who brought Joseph through betrayal, bondage, and brokenness is working behind the scenes of your life right now.

Observation — What Do We See?

- **Continuity of covenant:** Joseph's prophecy—*"God will surely visit you"*—links patriarchal promises to future deliverance.

- **Faith in instruction:** His request about his bones keeps Israel's hope mobile.

- **Pattern of visitation:** The Hebrew paqad denotes God's decisive intervention.

- **Death as transition:** His final act of faith shifts focus from personal success to generational fulfillment.

Keywords / Frequency / Emphasis

- **God will surely visit you** — certainty of divine continuity.

- **Bones / Carry out** — tangible faith in motion.

- **Promise / Canaan** — vision anchored beyond provision.

- **Finish / Perform / Complete** — divine perseverance.

Emphasis: Faith moves from **memory to movement**—from past favor to future fulfillment.

Interpretation — What Did It Mean Then?

For Israel, Joseph's dying words became a **roadmap of faith** through bondage. His bones symbolized **unburied belief**—evidence that hope still had an address.

Each generation could point to those bones and say, "We are not home yet."

Theologically, Joseph's confidence in God's visitation united the patriarchs' private walk with Israel's public destiny.

True faith leaves **instructions** for the next move of God.

Theological Principles

1. **God's Work Is Progressive:** The dream develops through generations.

2. **Faith Transcends Seasons:** What begins in one life continues in another.

3. **The Body Rests, the Word Runs:** Joseph's bones rested, God's Word advanced.

4. **Legacy Is Prophetic:** Obedient lives become maps for the wandering.

5. **Redemption Has Layers:** Joseph's story foreshadows Christ's.

6. **Heaven Keeps Records:** What God begins in you joins His eternal plan.

Wisdom Perspective — Mike Murdock on Completion and Purpose

Dr. Mike Murdock teaches, *"The proof of wisdom is the pursuit of completion.* "Joseph's life proved that principle. He refused to stop halfway through what God assigned. Every season—*the pit, Potiphar's house, the prison, and the palace*—became a classroom of completion.

Murdock also warns, *"Unfinished obedience is disobedience in disguise."* Joseph's greatness rested not only in his gift but in his follow-through. He managed his assignment until every divine detail was fulfilled.

As Murdock observes, *"Wisdom is the ability to recognize difference—the difference in people, timing, and opportunities."* Joseph discerned the difference between a **season of favor** and a **season of fulfillment,** between **a dream revealed** and **a dream realized.**

That discernment transformed opportunity into outcome and destiny into legacy.

Psychological Principles

- **Enduring Meaning:** Faith like Joseph's models transcendent continuity—the conviction that purpose outlives the person.

- **Symbolic Hope:** His bones act as a logotherapy symbol (Viktor Frankl)—a tangible reminder that meaning survives suffering.

- **Cognitive Reframing:** Joseph saw suffering as preparation, not punishment—the mark of true resilience.

- **Intergenerational Transmission:** Stories of endurance rewire hope; Joseph's narrative strengthened Israel's psyche in captivity.

Application — How Should We Respond?

- **Keep faith mobile:** Don't let success make you settle; carry vision into each season.

- **Leave prophetic instructions:** Guide those who come after you.

- **See death as delegation:** Pass the dream forward.

- **Trust God's timing:** The process may outlive you, but the promise will not.

- **Anchor your hope:** Keep your heart in Canaan even when your body is in Egypt.

Wisdom Keys

- God's promises are **generational**—what He starts in you speaks beyond you.

- Bones in a coffin can **preach** louder than words when faith lives inside them.

- Destiny delays are **divine designs.**

- True faith dies declaring, *"God will surely visit you."*

- The dream lives on when you refuse to let Egypt define your ending.

Reflective Questions:

1. Are you trusting God to finish what He started in your life?

2. What dreams have you buried that God wants you to carry again?

3. How does Joseph's confidence in God's visitation strengthen your faith?

4. Are you living with vision—even in a place that feels like Egypt?

5. What legacy of faith are you leaving for those who come after you?

Reflective Summary:

Joseph's life proves that destiny is not a destination—it's a journey of surrender.

He died in Egypt, but his heart was in the promise. He never confused Egypt's provision with Canaan's inheritance.

The dream lived on—through faith, through testimony, through memory.

And it still lives today—in you.

If God gave you the dream, He will finish what He started.

Keep walking. Keep believing. Keep preparing.

The dream is not dead—it's only beginning.

Prayer:

Father,

Thank You for being the Author and Finisher of our faith. Like Joseph, help us hold fast to the dream You've placed in our hearts. Even when the end seems far, let us walk by faith and not by sight.

Teach us to carry vision in obscurity and sow obedience for generations yet unborn. Let our bones testify of Your promises and our lives reveal Your glory.

We trust You to complete the work.

We believe the dream still lives.

In Jesus' name, Amen.

Chapter 12: The School of Preparation — Becoming the Minister Before the Ministry

"Study to shew thyself approved unto God, a workman that needeth not to be ashamed, rightly dividing the word of truth."

— 2 Timothy 2:15

Introduction — Before the Dream Becomes Visible

Every dream God gives has a classroom called preparation.

Before Joseph ruled, he served. Before David reigned, he watched sheep. Before Paul preached, he studied.

The season between calling and commissioning is where the minister learns to carry weight without collapsing under it.

Mike Murdock writes in The Assignment that "Preparation is proof you believe in the future."

Those who rush the process reveal that they doubt the promise. God's timing is not hesitation—**it is formation.**

If Joseph had been released too early, his gift would have outgrown his grace.

The same is true for every upcoming minister and leader today.

The Discipline of Study

Paul's charge to Timothy was not optional: *"Study to shew thyself approved unto God."* Study is worship. Study is warfare. Study is stewardship.

Ministers cannot live on borrowed revelation.

They must build a reservoir of truth deep enough to feed others when the crowd is hungry and silence is long.

Books, notes, and sermons are tools—but Scripture is the source.

To the up-and-coming minister:

- Read daily.

- Listen repeatedly.

- Learn relentlessly.

Fill your mind with the Word of God until your mind begins to think like the Word.

Mike Murdock writes in The Dream: "Your mind is the birthplace of every miracle." A disciplined mind produces a fruitful ministry.

Great ministers are not born on platforms—they are formed in private study, one revelation at a time.

The Discipline of Living Holy

Holiness is not a suggestion—it is the standard.

No amount of talent, charisma, or education can replace a clean life before God.

Paul told Timothy, *"Keep yourself pure."* **(1 Timothy 5:22).**

Holiness is the minister's invisible armor; it guards credibility, preserves anointing, and keeps spiritual authority intact. You can preach truth only when truth has first been allowed to cleanse you.

Holiness is more than moral restraint—it is complete devotion. It is the discipline of separating from the world's contamination and drawing near to God's character.

A holy vessel becomes a reliable vessel.

Mike Murdock once said, "You can't change what you tolerate."

Sin tolerated in private becomes scandal exposed in public.

If you want to walk in power, walk in purity. The Holy Ghost does not anoint rebellion, but He empowers those who pursue righteousness.

True holiness is not self-righteousness; it's **spiritual maturity.** It is humility in motion— walking *in repentance, self-control,* and *integrity* even when no one is watching.

As you prepare for ministry:

- Guard your eyes.

- Govern your thoughts.

- Protect your time.

- Keep your heart clean.

Holiness is the evidence that God has set you apart—not just to preach the Word, but to live it.

Spiritual Discipline — The Hidden Curriculum

Spiritual discipline is the bridge between revelation and realization.

Prayer, fasting, solitude, and obedience are not rituals; they are routines that make revelation sustainable.

Murdock reminds ministers in The Uncommon Minister: *"The secret of your future is hidden in your daily routine."*

Excellence in ministry begins long before anyone is watching.

A minister's schedule must reflect his seriousness.

- Study time must be guarded.

- Prayer time must be protected.

- Integrity must be practiced in secret.

And above all, serve others whenever possible.

Service keeps the heart soft, the ego crucified, and the spirit teachable.

Jesus washed feet before He sat at the right hand of the Father. True greatness still kneels before it leads.

The dream will never rise higher than the discipline—and holiness—that sustain it.

Observation — What Do We See?

- **Paul's mentorship of Timothy** shows that ministry growth is both spiritual and intellectual.

- **Joseph's years of obscurity** demonstrate that hidden seasons refine both character and competence.

- **Jesus' 30 years before public ministry** prove that divine silence is not divine absence.

- **Holiness and service** are the two foundations of sustainable leadership.

- **Preparation precedes promotion**—and purity protects both.

Keywords / Frequency / Emphasis

Study, Discipline, Holiness, Assignment, Preparation, Excellence, Service, Faithfulness.

Emphasis: The minister's first pulpit is his private altar; his first sermon is his lifestyle.

Interpretation — What Does It Mean?

Paul knew that gifted men without grounding collapse under the weight of public responsibility.

His counsel to Timothy—study, live pure, endure hardship, flee youthful lusts, pursue righteousness—was the blueprint for sustained ministry.

Preparation is not punishment; it is **proof of value.**

When God invests heavily in your development, it is because He intends to trust you greatly with influence.

Theological Principles

- **Divine Calling Requires Human Cultivation**. God plants potential, but man must water it through discipline.

- **Holiness Is Non-Negotiable.** God's presence dwells only in consecrated vessels.

- **Study Is a Form of Worship.** To handle Scripture correctly is to honor the Author.

- **Faithfulness Precedes Fruitfulness.** The call matures through obedience in small tasks.

- **Formation Before Function.** Ministry begins in devotion, not display.

- **Mentorship Is God's Method.** Timothy needed Paul; Elisha needed Elijah; every generation needs fathers and teachers.

Wisdom Perspective — Mike Murdock on the Minister's Assignment

From The Assignment: *"Your assignment is not decided by you; it is discovered through pursuit."* Upcoming ministers must discern not just where they want to serve, but whom they are called to serve.

From The Destiny: *"Preparation is the seed for promotion."* Every unseen act of obedience becomes currency in God's economy. When you study, pray, and serve in silence, heaven is recording.

From The Uncommon Minister: "What you make happen for others, God will make happen for you." Help your pastor. Support your church. Volunteer with excellence. Service in the small places prepares you for stewardship in the greater ones.

From The Dream: *"Dreamers who neglect discipline create nightmares."* Vision without structure collapses into frustration. Let your dream drive you to holiness and study, not to shortcuts.

Psychological Principles

- **Delayed Gratification:** Those who can wait faithfully mature emotionally and spiritually; patience strengthens identity.

- **Cognitive Immersion:** Immersing the mind in Scripture reshapes neural pathways—modern science calls this neuroplasticity.

- **Resilience through Routine:** Daily prayer, study, and holiness stabilize focus and emotional regulation under pressure.

- **Empathic Growth through Service:** Serving others develops emotional intelligence and dismantles self-centered ambition, producing ministers who lead from compassion.

- **Identity Formation:** Calling gives purpose; holiness gives stability. Together they create ministers who lead from wholeness, not performance.

Application — How Should We Respond?

1. **Make study and holiness a lifestyle.** Guard your purity and your doctrine equally.

2. **Stay busy in God's house.** Serve wherever you can—teach, mentor, visit, help, and encourage others.

3. **Invest in growth.** Read books that build character, not just charisma.

4. **Serve others joyfully.** Ministry begins with humility, not hierarchy.

5. **Protect your thought life.** The Word must fill the same mind the enemy tries to distract.

6. **Honor mentors and spiritual authority.** Submission invites covering; covering sustains calling.

7. **Embrace silence and seasons of testing.** Obscurity is God's workshop for holiness and authenticity.

Wisdom Keys

- Discipline is the scaffolding that holds up destiny.

- Holiness keeps the anointing fresh.

- Study until the Word becomes instinct.

- Serving others keeps your spirit safe from self-promotion.

- Preparation is never wasted—it's investment in divine trust.

- The anointing grows strongest in servants, not celebrities.

- You cannot pour from a dirty vessel— purity preserves power.

Reflective Questions:

1. How consistent is your personal study, prayer, and holiness?

2. In what ways is God training you through waiting and serving?

3. How does holiness protect your anointing?

4. Who are your mentors, and how do you honor their guidance?

5. How does service to others sharpen your sense of calling?

6. What practical steps can you take this month to deepen discipline and purity?

Reflective Summary:

The path to ministry excellence is paved with discipline, holiness, and service—not applause.

Every leader you admire once lived in a classroom called preparation. Study builds wisdom; holiness builds power; service builds compassion.

Together, they produce credibility that lasts.

To every upcoming minister: stay faithful. Keep your hands busy for God, your mind full of heavenly thoughts, and your heart pure.

Let the Word of God saturate you until it speaks through you.

Serve others with humility, live holy before God, and He will exalt you in due time.

When your season of manifestation comes, you won't have to chase opportunity—opportunity will recognize preparation, purity, and service.

Prayer:

Father,

Thank You for the privilege of study, service, and holiness. Help us to value preparation as much as promotion.

Teach us to be diligent students of Your Word and faithful servants in Your house. Form character before You display calling.

Let our discipline attract Your favor, and let our purity sustain it. Anoint this generation of ministers to walk in wisdom, holiness, and excellence.

May their dreams mature through devotion, their visions manifest through service, and their ministries reflect the heart and holiness of Christ.

In Jesus' name, Amen.

God Knows What He's About: A Poetic Reflection

To conclude this chapter, consider this powerful poem that echoes the very truth we've explored through Joseph's journey. It reminds us that the shaping of a servant is never random—it is heaven's intentional craftsmanship:

When God would shape a shepherd's heart, He leads him through the night;

He tempers steel with hidden fires and trains his hands for light.

He bends but does not break the soul He trusts to bear His grace;

He teaches love to outlast loss, and mercy to keep pace.

He quiets pride with patient days and sanctifies the wait;

He fits the servant for the yoke before He opens gates.

He fashions wisdom out of wounds and courage out of tears;

He writes a steadier song of faith than all the shouting years.

So walk the narrow, holy road and serve without applause—

In time the dream will bow to God, fulfilled for kingdom cause.

What He begins, He brings to pass; He never casts you out.

Take heart, O minister in training—God knows what He's about.

This poem is a reflection of every servant who has endured the silence of waiting, the burden of rejection, and the fire of refining. But through it all, God is producing something eternal—something ready.

Reflective Summary

Joseph's life ends, but the legacy continues. His bones would later be carried out of Egypt by a deliverer he never met, toward a promise he never personally stepped into. That's what happens when the call of God is on your life: it outlives you.

Delay does not cancel destiny. Silence does not mean absence. The dream still lives because the God who gave it is still faithful. Your call still stands.

To every reader who has felt forgotten, overlooked, or left behind in the ministry God once showed you—you are not abandoned. You are being prepared.

When God reveals what He's been doing in you, it will all make sense. The oil will flow. The door will open. And what felt like a delay will be recognized as divine design.

It is coming. What you thought was forgotten is about to be remembered. What you let go of is about to return, renewed. And what you prayed for in secret will be rewarded openly.

Prayer

Father,

Thank You for being faithful through the waiting, the silence, and the seasons of delay. Thank You for preparing us when we didn't even realize it. Help us to walk boldly in the call You've placed on our lives.

Forgive us for the times we doubted, gave up, or walked away. Today we return to the dream. We pick up the vision. We answer the call.

We declare: It is coming. The dream lives. The calling stands. And we are ready.

Thank You that what You start, You finish. And what You call, You equip.

In Jesus' name, Amen.

Epilogue: The Dream Still Lives—in You

Joseph's life may have ended in Egypt, but the dream God gave him never died. It lived on in his descendants, in the preservation of nations, and in the lineage that would one day bring forth the Messiah.

Joseph's story teaches us that when God gives a dream, He also provides *the strength, character, and grace* to carry it out.

You, reader, are part of that same legacy.

You may not wear a coat of many colors, or stand in Pharaoh's court—but you are called. You have been chosen. And though your road may look different, your God is the same.

The dream lives on—not in palaces or platforms, but in your persistence to believe when it's hard, to forgive when it's painful, and to serve when no one's watching.

You were born for such a time as this.

So, walk forward with boldness. Let every tear, trial, and test prove that God was building something greater than you imagined.

The pit could not hold Joseph. The prison could not break him. And the process did not disqualify him—it equipped him.

The same will be true for you.

The dream lives on… because you still believe.

Declaration of Faith

I believe that God has called me, chosen me, and is preparing me for a purpose greater than I can see.

I declare that delay is not denial. I trust God's timing and submit to His refining.

I will remain faithful in hidden seasons and serve with integrity wherever I am planted.

I will forgive those who hurt me, bless those who abandoned me, and walk in the love of Christ.

I receive the promise of God on my life—and I will not quit.

The dream shall live. I will live. And God shall be glorified in me.

Amen.

About the Author

Elder Joel Latimore Jr. is a Spirit-filled minister, author, and veteran of the United States Army. Having overcome years of rejection, hardship, and Spiritual refining, he carries a message of restoration, purpose, and Holy Ghost empowerment.

A graduate of Cleveland State University with a degree in Nonprofit Management, Elder Latimore is passionate about helping others walk into the fullness of their calling. He received upper-echelon training and ministry experience through the Church Of God In Christ, where he served faithfully under the leadership of Pastor James H. Bannerman at Greater Prayer Tower COGIC. He now serves under the leadership of Pastor Kennedy G. Lockhart at The Church, COGIC

His writings reflect his journey—marked by pain, shaped by obedience, and fueled by the fire of God. Elder Latimore lives each day with one mission: to awaken the dreams of those who feel forgotten, and to preach the uncompromising truth of God's Word with power and clarity.

Elder Joel Latimore Jr. is available for speaking and teaching engagements and can be reached by email: elderjoellatimore@yahoo.com or by calling (216) 501-3918.

www.ingramcontent.com/pod-product-compliance
Lightning Source LLC
Chambersburg PA
CBHW051257120626
46547CB00015B/1979